BODY TALK

Understanding the Secret
Language of the Body

BRUCE L. VAUGHAN

ARGUS COMMUNICATIONS A Division of **DLM,** Inc.
Allen, Texas 75002 U.S.A.

ACKNOWLEDGMENTS

The outstanding works of Robert Whiteside and John Shirley were extremely helpful in formulating a basis on which to build, but this book would never have been completed without the help of some very special people who assisted in its preparation. My personal thanks are given to Emmitt Crawford, who really co-authored this book. His command of the English language and his ability to put my thoughts into meaningful words make this book what it is.

Additional thanks go to my secretary, Helen Laznovsky, who took on the arduous task of typing this book from my bad handwriting. My thanks also go to the artistic talents of Kellum Brown, whose sketches make the book more easily understood. And special thanks to Barbara Klima for her insight.

Finally, thanks go to the people of the world whom I have studied over the years, who allowed me to stare at them, then interview them about their personalities, and who are responsible for the research and answers we have been able to determine. They are what this book is all about.

Designed by Tricia Legault

Cover illustration by Yoshi Miyake

Illustrated by Kellum Brown

First Edition

Copyright © 1982 by Argus Communications

Printed in the United States of America.

Argus Communications
A Division of DLM, Inc.
One DLM Park
Allen, Texas 75002 U.S.A.

International Standard Book Number: 0-89505-078-1
Library of Congress Catalog Card Number: 82-72496

0 9 8 7 6 5 4 3 2 1

Table of Contents

INTRODUCTION

Introduction

What is Body Talk?
Why is it important?
What can it do for me?
How do I use it?

These questions are some of the most frequently asked during our seminars. People are often shocked and amazed when they begin to understand the meaning and implications of this new science.

Body Talk is the term used here to describe what specific physical facial and body structures and characteristics reveal about your personality. Each specific indicator, such as the shape of eyebrows, lips, nose, or ears, has a direct relationship on the personality. When you understand the meaning of the specific indicators and begin to combine the characteristics of each, you will then begin to understand the basic framework of each individual's personality. From this information can be gleaned the nature of the person's thought patterns, probable responses to given circumstances, and a valuable insight into that person's life and life-style. This will allow you a better chance to relate to them. It gives you an inside track on knowing what makes people tick and how to communicate to their needs in a manner they will understand.

1

If we take the time to observe, we can learn most everything from one another. There is not a single thought in the human mind, whether tending toward good or evil, that does not have its distinct interpretor in the glance of an eye or in the expression of the muscles of the face. When Nature is permitted to express herself by the language of the face and body, she may be understood by all. Even those who cannot read a word can instantly read her signature and impression. The language of the face and body is universal and comprehensive to those aware of it. It is the shorthand of the mind and crowds a lot in a little space.

Body Talk is of tremendous value to us in this age of fast-paced, ulcerous living. Often we are dismayed and disillusioned at what is happening in the world we live in. It becomes increasingly more important in this complex, problematical society, therefore, to be understood and to relate and adapt to our changing world. These nonverbal communicators are an effective, accurate method of better understanding our fellow man, that we might communicate and relate much more wisely and efficiently in our daily lives.

Are you doubting? I would ask, then, that you look at your favorite pet. Your dog or cat communicates entirely on a nonverbal basis, yet we have very little difficulty understanding what it needs or wants. We merely have to observe its behavior. The same is true of humans. We need only apply these same techniques to truly understand mankind!

The use of Body Talk will also aid you in better understanding your own personality and will help you develop the skills wherein you may become aware of your own strengths and weaknesses as others may perceive them. Using Body Talk will help you express yourself to others better.

How often have you said something to someone else and knew he or she didn't really understand your meaning? In this situation you may have thought, "I know you think you heard what I said, but I'm not sure you know what I meant!" Proper understanding and use of Body Talk will assist you in speaking with your face and body and will enhance your ability to make yourself understood. Good communications are the keys to successful relationships, whether they be of a business, social, or personal nature.

As with other human behavioral sciences, the accuracy depends on the knowledge of the person applying the science. A knowledgeable person can achieve an accuracy rate of about 98 percent. Besides knowledge, some of the limiting factors are cosmetic surgery performed on the nose, a face lift, plucking of the eyebrows by women, wigs, dental plates, or a catastrophic illness such as a stroke. All these factors may affect the accuracy of the science. The trained eye, however, can usually spot other characteristics that will verify or indicate where the changes have taken place.

In some cases, although rare, the face may never catch up to a philosophical change in a life-style. Such instances may be due to a sudden major illness such as cancer or a heart attack. These factors account for the 2 percent inaccuracy of this as a science.

Assuming that the knowledge is absorbed and the traits verified and augmented by other characteristics, anyone can gain this insight into other people and their personalities.

My own personal philosophy is to help others understand each other. I believe that all of the world's problems could be solved if people would just relate better with their fellow man. Harmony and unity create growth. Dissidence and misunderstanding create havoc, chaos, and destruction. If just one person gains new insight and greater understanding of others through Body Talk, then my efforts will not have been in vain.

The face is the title page which heralds the contents of the human volume. In every face, either a history or prophecy may be revealed to every reflecting observer.

The Science of Body Talk

1
The Use of Body Talk in Your Personal Lives

Beneficial applications of Body Talk in our daily lives are many and varied. It is a very effective tool in understanding and solving social problems resulting from a breakdown of communications and relating to one another.

It is somewhat ironic that in most everything we do in life, we utilize some form of analytical process. When buying clothes, a home, food, jewelry, or even a car, we use some sort of deductive logic and reasoning. Yet when it comes to choosing our friends, lovers, or mates, we rely on emotional, gut-level feelings! In this formation of relationships, logic is a stranger.

I certainly do not intend to imply that emotional or gut-level feelings are wrong. In fact, quite the contrary. Without them, we have no base on which to build. However, if we temper these feelings and emotions with the knowledge of Body Talk, we will have a far greater chance of developing a successful relationship. In using Body Talk, we can avoid the disillusionment, disenchantment, and misunderstanding that so often accompany the greatest gift we have to give to others—that of self, love, respect, and mutual commitment.

Most authorities on human behavior and marital problems agree that if a single factor is involved in the breakup of a marriage or a relationship between lovers or friends, it would be the breakdown of communications between parties and a failure to relate on a one-to-one basis.

Consider, if you will, the case of the football player. Here is a rugged athlete, fond of physical contact and outdoor-type sports and recreation. He discovers a demure, somewhat pale and delicate, childlike, petite, beautiful young lady who is the epitome of female charm. He falls madly in love with her, desiring to place her on a pedestal, to love, cherish and protect this delicate flower of womanhood.

She, on the other hand, admires his great strength and virility. Reminiscent of her girlish concept of the gallant knight on the white charger, she longs to be secure and protected by him, wanting him to love, honor, and protect her so they may "live happily ever after." A beautiful and romantic love affair culminates in marriage based on emotion and feelings rather than anything resembling logic.

Here it might be appropriate to recall the old adage, "Love is a poor mariner; it languishes on long sea voyages." Though the fairy tales usually end with " . . . and they lived happily ever after," in reality, all too soon the honeymoon is over. The husband is often found in front of the television set watching football, or possibly out playing the game with friends on weekends. His desires are for the physical contact he had in school, the competitive challenges he faced and overcame, the weekends out camping in the wilderness, or the free and easy "locker room" talk he had with "the guys."

She, on the other hand, desires her fine operas, her reading of good literature, the attendance of a great play, or the gentle comfort of a fine dinner over candlelight and wine. In her love making, she desires the gentle approach and a great deal of prolonged foreplay leading up to the actual culmination of sex. She wants to be loved before loving, to be held and caressed and talked to romantically. He, in his rough and physical upbringing, is more interested in the "nitty-gritty." He wants to cut through all the pretense and get on with the game. It appears it is always the last seconds of the ballgame for him, and he is in a hurry to get it over with, often concerning himself with only his needs and not paying attention to hers.

She cannot physically endure the outdoor camping and the rough, manly type of living that he so enjoys. He, in turn, is bored to tears by the plays and concerts she wishes to attend. Neither is satisfied in the bedroom. Soon subtle unspoken differences begin to mount. A void develops between them. The basic differences in their personalities begin to manifest themselves with unspoken negative thoughts. She thinks he no longer loves her, while his mind is telling him that if she really loved him she would do the things he liked. Soon there is less and less communication between them, and neither really understands what is happening. The little nuisances and trials of daily routine begin the attrition of the bonds between them. Their marriage is falling apart.

We have all witnessed the end to this story. Opposites may attract, but it is common interests that will prolong and maintain a relationship. The failure of this relationship was not because love was not involved, but rather because the basic personalities were so different! The opposite physical characteristics and emotional feelings were not realized, there-fore, they could not be dealt with effectively, nor could they be related to appropriately. There have been many divorces of loving couples who could no longer stand living together.

Herein lies the applicability and relevance of Body Talk in our daily lives. Had the hypothetical couple described here been knowledgeable of this science, and used it to discover their basic differences as well as their similarities, they could have used logic and reason, along with their emotions, to gain a greater understanding of each other. Had they known of each other's desires and felt their love strong enough to survive their obvious differences, they could have made the appro-priate adjustments. At worst, they might have decided the compromises were too high a price to pay to further develop the relationship.

If in choosing a lover, mate, or friend we entail all the valid information possible to determine if both parties are compatible, and if acute differences do exist and the emotional attachment still remains, then at least a logical and sensible evaluation of all the factors may lead to a more amicable relationship on a one-to-one basis, and many pitfalls could be avoided.

Building a relationship on emotional feelings only is like building a house on a swamp. There is little wonder that our divorce rate is so high in this country. How little we really know about each other when we respond to each other with those two words of the marriage ceremony, "I do"!

In the marriage counseling I have done, it is apparent that most of the marriages in our society are at best tolerable, and those few couples who do find the true happiness that lasts throughout the years are truly blessed! I have so often heard people who have been married over twenty years still say that they do not understand their mates. The most successful marriages I have researched have been those in which the physical appearance of both parties is extremely similar. How often we have heard others say that people who have lived together for a long time grow to look like each other. I believe there is a semblance of truth in this statement, for as you think, so you look. Our features do change with time, and the influence of others affect our attitudes, which in turn affect our features.

So, if you are out looking for a relationship, whether it be one of friendship or love, temper your feelings with this knowledge, and your chances of building a successful relationship will improve tremendously.

2
Using Body Talk in Business

The use of Body Talk in business is so diversified that it is difficult to know where to begin. It is applicable to every phase of the business world—from management to the most common of laborers, from large corporations to the one-person business. Anywhere there is a need to relate to others, this science can improve that relationship or communication.

From an employer-employee standpoint, it can be used to screen applicants for better jobs or help managers better understand how their employees are motivated. It is the wise, successful company that realizes that motivation is as individual as people themselves. And the job applicant can decide if he or she could work successfully with a prospective new boss.

For far too long we have tried to motivate people by groups. The sales contests that offer a trip for the winner only motivate a percentage of those vying for it. The large bonus that many companies use as a means of motivating people also only covers about 50 percent of the people involved. It is difficult to establish different motivations for different people within the same framework on the job; however, the very successful companies have discovered just how to do this. It has resulted in far less turnover in personnel and far greater efficiency in work output.

In the field of sales, this science is a must. The ability to relate to a customer or client in a selling situation is paramount to success. Education and counseling are fields in which Body Talk may be used to great advantage. It is almost a must in marriage counseling. Everyone dealing with the general public can use this knowledge effectively to improve their life-styles. Waitresses and waiters may increase their tips by using this same knowledge.

Much of the work I currently do involves using the knowledge of reading people's faces to assist attorneys in jury selection. This has proven to be quite a challenge, and I am greatly rewarded in knowing that in some small way I have aided justice. How valid is this work? We have yet to lose a case! Selecting the best possible jury for an attorney, giving him or her a complete breakdown on each individual juror and how each can be better understood taxes this science to its utmost, yet it still shines through unblemished.

Working with troubled teens is another aspect of Body Talk that merits comment. In most cases, the problems stem from lack of communications between the teen and the parents. Again, far too often we are unable to communicate on the level of the teenager. Why? Because we do not understand their motivations or their needs from *their* point of view. We insist on forcing them to attempt to understand us on *our* level of motivation and needs. Thus we create the so-called generation gap. By using the basics of Body Talk, we can automatically have a greater knowledge of what these same teenagers need, as well as a better method of understanding them and communicating with them. What a tremendous boon to society this would be. It will also help them to better understand us.

So, what does all this mean? I believe it means that learning how to read people's faces will help you relate, communicate and will aid you in your business and social life. Regardless of tangible benefits derived, it is an interesting study and fun to apply. But before we begin to learn the different characteristics, take a minute or two to answer the simple self-evaluation test which follows. Be as honest with yourself as you can, for the only person who needs to see the test is you. If you don't understand a category, just skip it and go on to the next. Some of the traits will not have a lot of meaning until you have finished reading the book. But again, you are the only person who will see this test, so you have nothing to fear. The purpose of the test is for self-growth and has no negative connotations or wrong answers. Reread the test after you have finished reading the book to check your accuracy.

Have fun—and may you all "read" people better from this point forward.

TEST YOUR KNOWLEDGE OF YOURSELF

As Others See You
From a Nonverbal Standpoint

*(Rate yourself from **1** to **10** on each of the traits listed below.*
*1 equals **LOW**, and 10 equals **HIGH** on any trait score.)*

NOTE: There is no right or wrong score to any trait, nor is there a good or bad score to attain. This test is for your own knowledge and self-understanding. It is used as a comparison between your present impressions and those gained after understanding the keys to nonverbal communication. An extra column is presented so you may score someone else you wish a better understanding of in relationship to you.

PERSONALITY TRAIT	MEANING of TRAIT (if necessary)	SCORE 1 TO 10		
		Yourself before reading book	Yourself after reading book	Someone else important
Ego				
Self-confidence				
Basic motivation	Security, recognition, money, survival, people, acceptance (circle one)			
Self-reliance				
Impulsiveness				
Adventurousness	Desire for adventure			
Need to dominate	The need to be the leader			

PERSONALITY TRAIT	MEANING of TRAIT (if necessary)	SCORE 1 TO 10		
		Yourself before reading book	Yourself after reading book	Someone else important
Stubbornness				
Authoritative ability	How well you handle authority			
Dramatic sense	How dramatically you view life			
Need for harmony				
Emotional appearance	Automatic reactions to emotional things			
Helpfulness to others				
Money management				
Decision making				
Analytical ability				
Tolerance of rules				
Criticalness				
Skepticism				
Open-mindedness				
Generosity				
Conciseness				
Tact				

PERSONALITY TRAIT	MEANING of TRAIT (if necessary)	SCORE 1 TO 10		
		Yourself before reading book	Yourself after reading book	Someone else important
Self-expression				
Extrovert				
Introvert				
Physical insulation	Ability to withstand pain			
Aloofness				
Meet people easily				
Ambitious				
Perfectionist				
Systematic approach				
Concern for detail				
Worrier or fussbudget				
Sense of humor				
Carefulness				
Possessiveness				
Deceitfulness				
Procrastination				

PERSONALITY TRAIT	MEANING of TRAIT (if necessary)	SCORE 1 TO 10		
		Yourself before reading book	Yourself after reading book	Someone else important
Vanity				
Patience				
Impatience				
Objective nature	Overcome obstacles as you go			
Subjective nature	Think things through before acting			
Idealistic in nature				
Realistic in nature				
Curiosity				
Accident Prone				
Handle pressure well				

FACE LANGUAGE

Before reviewing the face language portion of these notes, it is necessary to evaluate their importance compared to the other sciences. Wherever there is a conflict in facial characteristics versus body types of somatotyping, always trust the face language first. The best approach is to look for the augmenting traits to see if there may have been a recent change. If the augmenting traits are not there, then proceed with caution, because this usually indicates a change has taken place.

3
Face Language

What I refer to as "Face Language" is a relatively new field in the sciences of human behavior. It had its beginning in ancient times, mostly in the Orient, and has been called physiognomy by most students. This was the basic beginning of all nonverbal communication studies. In more recent times, in the mid-1940s, a lawyer named Edward V. Jones sought a more proficient understanding of both his clients and his juries. By close scientific examination of different classes of people in common endeavors, Jones noticed each had a distinct facial characteristic. From this preliminary concept he was able to develop much information, and many basic patterns began to emerge. Robert Whiteside studied Jones's findings and with continued analyzation of those findings, soon began to correlate them and augmented his own findings into what is now called Personology. Whiteside founded the Interstate College of Personology.

Personology or Face Language is the science of interpreting personality traits by their relationship to facial structure and features. It is the study of physical trait relationships (facial features) to personality traits. It is one of the brightest stars on the horizon of human behavioral sciences. The face is the mirror of the mind. Your thoughts become etched on your face, reflecting an image of your mind's actions. "As a man thinketh in his heart, so is he." If you wish to know a peoples' real thoughts, look into and study their faces, for they can control their words more easily than their expressions. For those knowledgeable in face language, a good face is the best letter of recommendation.

Before looking at the basic facial structure indicators, it must be pointed out that almost everything is judged by degree. We have chosen to use a one-to-ten scale where applicable. This takes time and practice to develop the ability to gauge where on the scale a particular trait registers. It can be done, however, and as in most endeavors, the more you use this science, the greater your accuracy will be in understanding others.

It is also important to note that a single trait does not indicate an exact personality trait. You must look for the augmenting traits to any given trait to assure yourself the accuracy. The overall picture must be considered, and the augmenting traits must reinforce the validity of the basic trait. The more augmenting traits present, the greater or stronger the basic trait. An example of this is the trait indicating optimism, which is the turned-up corners of the mouth, as is so aptly shown in the thespian masks. The turned-up corners indicate a basic outlook of optimism, but it is usually reinforced by the addition of humor lines, sparkling eyes, and a happy countenance. If the augmenting traits are not there, then further exploration of other traits should be done.

Remember, no two faces are alike, even in identical twins. Each and every one of us is different. Face language is only an aid to understanding, not an attempt to categorize people into any set pattern. Also, it is important to know that as the personality changes, so does the facial structure. It does take time for changes to manifest themselves in the face after the personality has changed its outlook, so this science is not a panacea, merely a tool to be used to help you understand others.

There are also exceptions to every rule, and just as sure as life itself, you will eventually run into someone who doesn't fit his or her face language. It has happened to me, and I expect it will happen to all of you at some time or another. When this does happen, learn from it if you can, for it will help you in understanding others later on.

4
Dominant Versus Recessive Sides
The Left-Right Differences

At this point it is well to observe that in many people you will find a difference in the structure of the face on the left and right side. Most indicators do have a basic left-right difference that requires some analysis. Basic left-right differences occur when an individual assumes two separate patterns of thought and behavior corresponding to distinct aspects of their attitudes associated with public and private life or in business and home life. Some people display certain basic traits in business or public and different traits privately in their home life. These differences will be indicated by differences in size, shape, or position of the respective face-language indicators on one side of the face. An illustration of this would be a person who publicly displays a very friendly, aggressive nature, but privately, at home, would display a shy, retiring, passive nature. Someone who is very self-reliant in business, confident and aggressive, may be very dependent, insecure, and less confident at home, or vice versa.

Our body, as previously noted, is a product of our every thought. The thought must first be born before every action. The thought transmitted through the brain instructs the body to function and to perform an action. Consistent and repeated patterns of thought etch into the face a pattern or design consistent with the thought patterns. Students of physiology will be familiar with the concept of neuromuscular pathways that form the foundation for the development of habits. Thus the face becomes a road map of the mind, showing the direction and nature of the thought patterns. Therefore, a concentration of thought in a single aspect of life, such as business, will display a mirrored image to the thought patterns on the face. When one assumes a different attitude and different thought patterns regarding one aspect of life that is different from another, the same difference will be noted on the dominant side of the face. The facial indicators of face language will correspond to this difference. Concentration of thought, time, and effort devoted to a certain area of life will alter the facial structure on the dominant side of the face.

If one spends more time and effort concentrating on business or public life, the dominant side will show the indicators typical of the personality traits displayed in the business life of the individual. In that same individual, the recessive side would indicate the personality traits consistent with attitudes and behavior regarding the private or home life.

The recessive side indicates an area of life in which a lesser degree of concentration of time, thought, and effort is expressed. The dominant side indicates an area of life in which a greater degree of concentration of thought, time, and effort is expressed.

The recessive side of the face indicates the recessive side of the personality, which is the side of life that receives the least amount of thought time. This difference of thought time can range from 51 to 49 percent or from 99 to 1 percent, depending upon the different thought processes occurring on each side. Left-right differences can indicate a difference in concentration on your home life or business life, corresponding to the difference in attitude and action displayed in

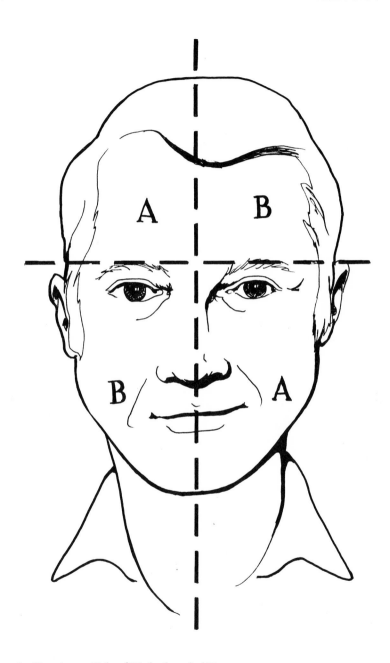

A. Dominant Side of Right-handed Person
B. Dominant Side of Left-handed Person

each. In some cases this difference may indicate a secret or hidden aspect of the personality that is being suppressed. This suppressed factor may be secret desires or emotions not expressed either at home or at work.

To interpret the basic left-right differences, we must first establish which is the dominant side of the face and which is the recessive side. If you are left-handed, the right side of the face is the dominant side. If you are right-handed, the left side is the dominant side. The dominant side of the face begins at the eyebrow horizontally and vertically down the middle of the face. The upper-right-hand side of the forehead relates to the left-lower side of the face and conversely for the upper-left side.

One can usually determine, through observation and conversation, whether a person is right- or left-handed. This provides the knowledge to determine the dominant side. For instance, a right-handed person usually wears a watch on the left wrist. Observation of details such as this will aid in determination of the dominant side. It is always helpful to know what a person does for a living also, since this is an important clue to the area of life most likely to receive more concentration of thought time. If, for instance, the person is known to be a public speaker or perhaps a politician and has a marked difference of left-right traits such as rhetoric lines, self-expression lines, and humor lines on the dominant side, then you may safely assume that the left-right differences indicate a greater concentration of thought time and effort on public life.

Remember, the dominant side is the one that receives the majority of thought time and concentration. By analyzing somatotyping characteristics and other facial indicators displayed by individuals, supported by what you can learn through conversation and observation of the person, you can usually determine which side of their personal, private, business, or public life they spend more time and concentration of thought processes. Generally, if you know the occupation of the individual, this information will provide the key to interpreting the basic left-right differences. Once you have determined the dominant side and know which side of the person's thought processes receives more concentration, you may then observe the recessive side to interpret the different personality traits expressed on the other side by the facial indicators. A person may be very aloof in the business world and very open and friendly in private life, or vice versa.

Understanding and interpreting basic left-right traits requires more analysis than other traits, but with practice this can be mastered, and understanding these traits will elicit a more in-depth understanding of the personality. Usually, left-right traits manifest according to the relationship to personality traits associated with home/work relationships. In the case of children, it would be the relationship of home and school. Housewives would illustrate the relationship of home and social activities. This may be the difference between a private side and an open, public side. The degree of difference in left-right traits corresponds proportionately to the difference in life-styles expressed by each side of the personality.

Beware . . . caution must be taken on certain traits. When cosmetic surgery has happened, such as a "nose bob" or other such surgery, then the trait must be discarded. If a person has had major philosophical changes in attitudes, such as could be caused by a heart attack, then the face language may not be accurate. Also, women can sometimes change their facial language with the aid of cosmetics; however, we usually find that when they do, they are attempting to change their personalities to match.

Remember, there are no two faces exactly alike. Each face is like a fingerprint—totally unique to its owner. It is the ability to view the combinations and their degrees that allows for a complete understanding of a person's personality.

5
Facial Indicators

The eye has been called the mirror of the soul, and this has a great deal of meaning to it. The eye is the first trait we look at. It draws our immediate attention to it. It also gives the most meaningful information. In studying nonverbal communication, the eye takes the number-one spot in importance. Many of the more popular cliches we use concern the eye, and with justification. Such comments as "he appears shifty-eyed," or "she looks worried," or "he has that strained look about him," or "she looks greedy," all pertain to the eye. Much can be learned about someone's personality by being observant of the eyes.

Large Irises

The larger a person's iris, the more emotionally expressive that person will be. These people think with their hearts more so than their heads, and will relate emotionally to situations automatically. They are easily hurt by others' comments, and they show it. They are sentimental in nature.

Small Irises

The small-eyed people are more matter of fact in nature and conceal their emotions from others. They usually think with their heads rather than their hearts. They are somewhat tough minded and can be self-centered. They are often accused of being cold hearted when in fact they are just hiding their emotions.

Eyes Wide Open

Wide-open eyes indicate people who see most everything that goes on around them. They have good peripheral vision and tend to notice details. Because their eyes are wide open, they tend to react quicker to situations than those whose eyes are squinted or partially closed.

Eyes Partially Closed or Squinted

Partially closed or squinted eyes indicate people who are channeling their thoughts. They have the ability to focus their attention on what they feel is important. (Note: Do not confuse this with squinting against sunlight or being nearsighted.) Occasionally they will miss the things that happen right around them.

Large Iris

Small Iris

Wide-Open Eyes

Squinting Eyes

Eyes Slanting Upward from the Nose Toward the Ear

The greater the degree of upward slant to the eyes, the less critical the person will be. These people are easy to get along with, and rarely will they criticize another. They believe in live and let live.

Eyes Slanting Downward from the Nose Toward the Ear

The greater the degree of slant downward from the nose toward the ear, the more critical in nature the person. Those with eyes slanting downward are quick to notice flaws and discrepancies. This is a good trait as long as they are being paid to be critical. Such occupations as proofreader or quality control inspector almost require this type of eye.

Eyes Set Close Together

These people have lower tolerance levels and tend to go by the book. They are often perfectionists and are hard to please. They have a tendency to want to change the world and will accept other people's problems, even when they are not asked to. They are often accused of being narrow-minded.

Wide-Set Eyes

The wider the distance between the eyes, the greater the tolerance of others. This pertains to how these people view the rules. If it is necessary to bend or break the rules, the wide-set eyes will do so with less guilt. They, too, believe in live and let live.

Eyes Slanting Upward Toward Ear

Slanting Downward Eyes

Narrow-Set Eyes

Wide-Set Eyes

33

Lots of Visible Eyelid

This indicates a direct actionist, a doer who makes things happen. They are capable of making decisions quickly and getting right to the heart of a situation. They often will leap before looking, and when being sold something they will look for the benefits of a product, as opposed to the specifications or technical information.

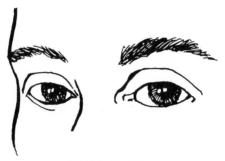

Visible Eyelids

No Visible Eyelid

These are the analytical people who want to know all the details. They deal in facts and figures and take a step-by-step approach toward most everything they do. Their concern for detailed information often keeps them from making fast decisions. When doing businesss with these types of people, be sure you have "all your ducks in order" before you start to deal with them.

No Visible Eyelids

Probably the most important nonverbal communicators to look for are the indicators for pressure and problems. These signs are found in the eye. The look you are hoping to find in a person is the clear, nonworried, steady gaze you will find on most people. This look exposes most of the iris (colored portion) of the eye, but not all the iris. There is usually a small portion at the top and bottom of the iris that is covered by the eyelid. If you see whites above or below the iris, this is an indication of problems. Naturally, we are referring to viewing the person in a relaxed state, as opposed to attempting to create this effect.

Glassy Eyed

When you view persons who appear extremely glassy eyed and who also seem to have a blank stare to their appearance, you are seeing people who are not with you in their mental state. They are elsewhere in thought, and if you ask them to do something for you, or give them a project, they will probably do things wrong, or at best, make some minor mistake. This condition is caused by the flow of adrenalin in the system and is an indication of lack of attention to anything other than their personal situation.

Blank Stare

Whites Showing Below the Iris

This is an indication of pressure in a person's life. The greater the degree of white showing, the greater the degree of pressure present. This indicates persons who have problems and do not know where to go to find the solutions. They are under tremendous pressure, and often they are looking for a place to unload these problems. The Japanese call this *san paku* (three whites). When you view this in other people, be careful not to add further to their already burdened situation. Try to help them if they are friends or close relations and you feel you can be of assistance. Just being aware of the situation will help a great deal.

Whites Showing Below Iris

Whites Below One Iris but Not the Other

I refer to this as *one-eyed san paku*. The appearance is whites under one eye, but not the other. This indicates pressure problems of the same magnitude as under both eyes; however, it pertains to only one half of the person's life-style. This is usually found in the difference between home life and business life, or public life versus private life. When there is a difference of personality between the two, it will often show up in the difference between the left side of the face and the right side of the face, as mentioned earlier in Chapter 4. When pressure mounts in one area but not the other, it creates tension in the muscle structure and causes one eyeball to shift slightly upward. This is usually not enough to affect a person's vision; however, it does affect both depth perception and peripheral vision, and thus creates "an accident looking for a place to happen." When this is visible, a person is likely to bump into things and in general have very poor depth perception when changing lanes in traffic, or coming to a halt at a stop sign. Thus we say a person is accident prone in this condition. This is the first thing to look for in yourself when you get up in the morning, and if you see this condition in existence, then treat that day with extra caution, until you eliminate the cause of the pressure.

Whites Below One Iris Only

Whites Below the Eyes with Only Half the Iris Showing

If you see the whites below the iris and less than two-thirds of the iris showing, be extremely cautious around these people. Not only are they under extreme pressure, but added to that, they are trying to hide something. When the eyelid comes down to conceal part of the iris like the picture shows and the eyeball has drawn up in the socket, you can be sure these people are hiding something they do not want discovered, and are under intense pressure to keep it hidden.

Whites Below Eyes, Half of the Iris Visible

Whites Below, Half the Iris Showing, and Glassy Eyed

When this combination is apparent, run, don't walk to the nearest exit! This combines pressure with trying to hide something, and not being with you in mental thought. *This*

37

person has psychotic tendencies! Any little thing could set this person off, and often he or she will commit acts of violence as a means to escape reality. This person could turn on the best of friends under this condition.

Whites Below, Half of the Iris Showing, and Glassy Eyed

Three Whites—Left, Right, and Above the Iris

If you see this combination be extremely cautious. This is what I call the psychopathic killer eye. It is indicative of a person who is attempting to gain power over you. It is also an indication of a diabolical nature and is dangerous to be around. Fortunately this seldom-seen condition is rare.

Three Whites Visible

Eyes Set Deeply in Sockets

Eyes set deeply into their sockets, giving the appearance as being set deep into the head, show how concerned the person is with himself or herself. The deeper set into the head the eyes are, the more self-centered the person is. This trait will change with people's attitude toward themselves. This is usually a low self-esteem form of concern rather than a high-ego type of concern. These people will question almost everything in relation to themselves and usually wonder why these things happen to them. They often feel that the world is against them and worry about how they can cope with life.

The opposite of this is the "bug-eyed" person whose eyes appear to bulge out of the sockets. These people have a very high self-esteem and high ego, and they often take a "know-it-all" attitude.

Inner Eyes Level with Each Other

When you measure how level the inner eyes are with each other, you can determine how people make their judgments. Looking at the point of the tear duct area and seeing whether one side sits higher than the other tell the viewer how that person will make major decisions. If the eyes are straight across from each other, then that person will base decisions on facts and logic. The more offset they are, the more that person will depend on feelings and emotions to make major decisions, rather than using facts and logic. The feelers and emotional people are in the majority in this trait.

Level—Facts and Logic

Unequal—Feelings and Emotions

Indented Area (front view) by the Eyes

Viewing the face from the front, if you see an indentation by the eyes, this is an indication of the trait for tact. The greater the indentation, the greater the degree of tact. This will be seen quite readily on those people who deal with troubled people, such as doctors, members of the clergy, or counselors. No indentation in this area is average, and if there is a bulge in this area, this is considered a sign of bluntness.

Indented Area by Eyes

Eye Contact Avoidance

There are no specific traits for honesty or integrity, since this would depend on a belief system. Even the professional thief has a code of integrity among peers. There are traits for dishonesty, however, and these are readily seen. The first trait that is apparent is the shifty-eyed look. A shifty-eyed person cannot look you in the eye when talking to you and will not look at any given thing for any length of time. This is not to be confused with the person who is in fear of you and cannot look you in the eye because of that fear, such as during a job interview. The second thing to look for is the deceitful eye, or the type of squint that says, "I'm hiding." This is often seen on the unscrupulous salesperson who is trying to sell you something other than what is being represented.

Crow's Feet

Crow's feet are an indication of a good sense of humor and cannot be erased with cream! If you laugh a lot and have a good sense of humor, these lines will develop. Outdoor people who squint a lot into the sun also develop these lines.

Crow's Feet

Extended Crows Feet

Lines that start from under the eye and move outward and then downward, over the cheekbone, are known as rhetoric lines. They indicate a love of good word usage and good English, as well as a desire for the well-turned phrase. These lines will appear in good public speakers, politicians, and good English teachers.

Extended Crows Feet

41

Flat Eyebrows

Flat eyebrows indicate people who like a challenge. They have an ability to work in harmony and teamwork with others. Harmony is a must in their lives, and they will usually have a love of the esthetic things in life such as music, art, and literature. Challenge is a prime motivator, however, confrontation will not work with these people.

Rounded, Half-Moon Eyebrows

This eyebrow is very similar in nature to the flat eyebrow. The basic differences are (1) they do not need quite as much of a challenge in their lives as the very flat-eyebrowed people do and (2) they have an ability to intermesh things or people. Often this is called the mechanical eyebrow because of the ability to put things together.

The Highly Arched Eyebrow

This is known as the dramatic eyebrow. It indicates people who view life very dramatically, with a flair for seeing everything as though they were on stage. They usually view life as a whole rather than in pieces. They have an excellent sense of timing and color coordination. They are very descriptive in their speech and actions and usually will extricate themselves verbally from difficult situations rather than resort to physical violence.

The Inverted Vee Eyebrow

This eyebrow is similar to the dramatic eyebrow, with the differences showing up in their ability to organize. The inverted-vee people are excellent organizers, but they often are not very good on the detailed follow-through. This type of person would rather lead than follow and can sometimes be very difficult to work with. They will rarely admit to being wrong, usually presenting an excuse.

Flat Eyebrow

Half-Moon Eyebrow

Highly Arched Eyebrow

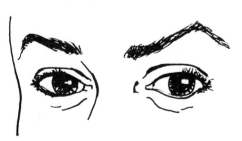

Inverted Vee Eyebrow

The Eyebrow That Is Flat on the Bottom and Rounded or Arched on the Top

This combination indicates a person who is organized or dramatic in nature, and combines those traits with the traits for harmony and challenge. The degree of arch will indicate the organizational ability. This eyebrow is most often seen on successful business people.

Eyebrows That Sit Close to the Eye

The closer the eyebrow sits to the eye, the more easygoing the person is. These people, friendly and informal in nature, are very down to earth—what you see is what you get. They meet people easily and have a multitude of friends.

Eyebrows That Sit High Over the Eye

The higher the eyebrow sits over the eye, the more reserved and aloof the person is. These people are selective, discriminating, and more formal with others. They usually demand and get respect from others. Often they may appear to be shy or timid, when in reality they are just being their normal, cautious self. There is often a hidden side to their personality that they do not wish to expose to the general public.

Eyebrows That Come Close Together at the Center of the Face

The closer the eyebrow comes together at the nose, the easier it is for that person to meet people. Conversely, the farther apart they are, the more distant or reserved a person will tend to be. (Note: Women will often pluck this portion of the eyebrow close to the nose; therefore, this may not be an accurate appraisal with females.)

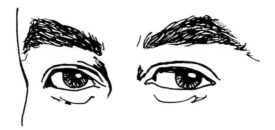

Combination Eyebrow

Eyebrows Close to the Eye

Eyebrows High Over the Eye

Eyebrows Close Together at Center

Lines Between the Eyebrows

The lines found between the eyebrows are called the fussbudget or worry lines. They indicate a person who worries. They also indicate a person who is somewhat of a perfectionist, and they can indicate a person concerned with time. The deeper the lines, the greater the degree of concern. Looking at other traits will usually indicate where the area of concern is.

Worry Lines   No Lines Between Eyebrows

No Lines Between Eyebrows

A lack of lines between the eyebrows indicates a live-and-let-live attitude. These people are not overly time conscious and often will be late for appointments.

Flat Area in the Worry-Line Area

The trait for carefulness is a depressed or flat area in the worry-line area. The greater the degree of flatness in this area, the greater the degree of caution in the individual. These people move very slowly to change and tend to follow set patterns that have proven beneficial to them, without trying to improve with new ideas.

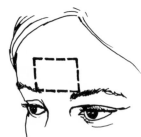

Flat Area in the Worry-Line Area

The Hook Nose

The hook nose is an indication of people who relate to money. These people know the value of a dollar and usually know how to make money easily. They are excellent business people and they rarely get taken in matters of finance. When they are purchasing something, they know how to gain the best value for the dollar spent.

The Hook Nose

The Straight or Roman Nose

People with the straight or Roman nose know the value of a dollar and generally expect to be paid for their efforts. They handle money well and will most always look for a "deal." They shop for value most of the time, but can on occasion be taken when their own greed makes them buy that "special deal" that turns out to be a rip-off. They often spend more time shopping around in an effort to save money than the amount of savings justifies.

The Straight or Roman Nose

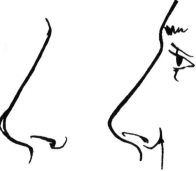

The Concave or Turned Up Nose

The people with the turned up noses are considered the helpers of the world. They often do not handle money well, since it usually is not their prime motivator. These people will give you the shirt off their back if they like you, and will do most anything to help you if asked. A pat on the back goes a long way with these people. Too often people take advantage of their helpful nature and abuse their friendship by using them.

Turned Up Nose

The Combination Nose

This is the combination of the hook nose and the helper or turned up nose. It appears to have a small hump in it, then the tip is turned up. This combination ties together the helpful nature with good money sense. These people know value and do not always buy the cheapest item, but rather will purchase the best value that will help them the most. They understand the workings of money, but do not let it rule their lives. They know how to make their money work both for themselves and for the good of others.

Combination Nose

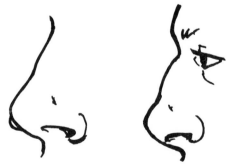

Combination Nose—Straight and Turned Up

This nose combines the good price and helper traits. These people still are very concerned about money and getting a good price on what they buy, but they also like helping others because that gives them recognition. They rarely help others with money, but rather with their time.

**Combination Nose—
Straight and Turned Up**

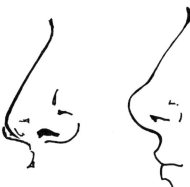

Size of the Nose Tip

The nose tip size is the measurement for curiosity. The more bulbous the nose tip, the greater the curiosity. These people seem to have a knack for being in the right place at the right time, to know what is going on.

Small Nose Tip   **Large Nose Tip**

Angle of the Nose Tip to the Base of the Nose

Viewing the nose from the side, if it appears to angle upward, you are seeing people who are open-minded. They will often take things at face value, and because of their open-mindedness, they are often taken advantage of. They will

49

appear gullible, because of their desire not to be skeptical. The person whose nose is not angled upward or downward is in the average classification. They tend to take a show-me attitude and often do not take things at face value, unless proven to them. They are not overly skeptical, just cautious. The greater the downward turn to the nose, the greater the degree of skepticism. Those with the tip turned down will doubt most everything and will rarely accept anything at face value. They tend to doubt first and wait until you prove everything, and even then they may not believe what you are saying. The extreme of this trait are the true cynical persons who don't believe anything, including themselves.

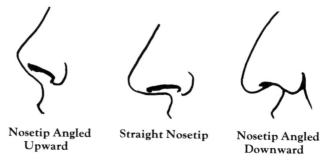

Nosetip Angled Upward   **Straight Nosetip**   **Nosetip Angled Downward**

Widely Flared Nostrils

The greater the degree of flair to the base of the nostrils, the greater the degree of self-reliance. These people usually are self-starters and relate well to many people. They are aggressive and will most always feel in command of themselves.

Widely Flared Nostrils

Narrowly Flared Nostrils

Narrowly flared nostrils is an indication of low self-reliance. These people need at least a single one-on-one relationship in their lives. They need close ties with a loved one or with family, and if they are not satisfied in their love life, they will usually break the connection *before* they stray or look for a replacement. They rarely stray from the fold if their mates keep them happy.

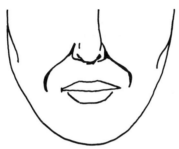

Narrowly Flared Nostrils

Distance Between Bottom of Nose and Top of Upper Lip

The distance between the bottom of the nose and the top of the upper lip shows the amount of vanity a person has. The shorter this distance, the greater the vanity will be in that person. Vanity refers to how well people look, especially in their opinion of what others think about them. To the vain person, looks are of extreme importance.

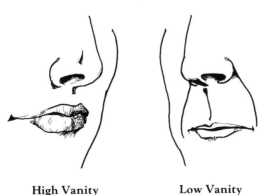

High Vanity   **Low Vanity**

Wide or Large Mouth Versus Small or Narrow Mouth

The size of the mouth is an indication of how extroverted or introverted the person is. The wider the mouth, the more extroverted the person will be. Conversely, the smaller the mouth, the more reserved or introverted an individual will be.

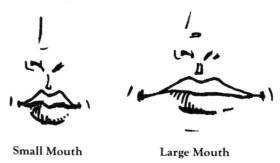

Small Mouth   Large Mouth

Thick Lips

The thickness of the lips indicates the basic generosity of the personality. The thicker they are, the more generous in nature the person. This generosity is in their actions and does not necessarily mean generosity with their money, though it can mean generosity with money if other traits so indicate. It is applied basically to their time and to being generous of themselves. The thickness of the upper lip can be indicative of generosity with words, and the thickness of the lower lip indicates generosity of actions.

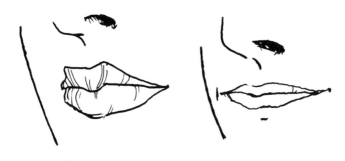

Thick Lips   Thin Lips

Thin Lips

Thin lips indicate conciseness. The thin-lipped people are more to the point and do not like their time wasted. They are not overly generous in nature and strive for efficiency. They usually do not say much, preferring short, to-the-point statements, rather than long, drawn-out replies. These people are conservative in nature.

Cautionary Note: If a person wears dentures, even partials, or has had perodontal work done, then this thick- or thin-lip trait must be discounted. Dentures cause a change in the muscle structure use, thereby changing this trait.

Firm, Angular, Wedge-shaped Jaw

The indication for determination is a firm, angular, wedge-shaped jaw. The greater the degree of wedge shape, the greater the degree of determination. This is also the mark of stubbornness. Once these people make up their minds, it is difficult to change them.

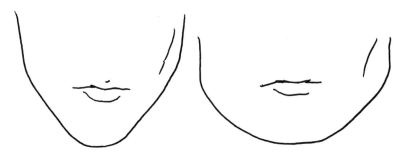

The Angular Wedge-shaped Jaw   Squarer, More-rounded Jaw

The Squarer, More-rounded Jaw

The more rounded or squarer the jaw, the more flexible the person. These people are executive in nature and are capable of making changes in their decisions before they reach that self-destruct state. They are more forgiving in nature. (Many political leaders fit this description.)

High Cheekbones

High cheekbones are the trait for adventurousness. When you see the high cheekbone, you are seeing a high degree of adventurousness in the personality. The higher the cheekbone, the greater the desire for adventure. How that desire is fulfilled is determined by other traits.

High Cheekbones

Authoritative Lines

Authoritative lines start either at the corner of the mouth or sometimes are a continuation of the self-expression lines. They define the chin area quite clearly. The ability to *handle* authority is measured by looking at the chin structure or chin lines. This is the ability to handle responsibility and direct others when asked to do so. We measure this as follows: Draw an imaginary line straight down the face from the outside edge of the iris of both eyes to below the chin. Now look for the outline of the chin. (Caution: We are looking at the chin only, not including the jaw.) If the chin line falls inside of the imaginary line, you are seeing someone who does not want authority. If the line is equal to the chin line, then you are seeing someone who can handle authority when asked to do so, but who does not seek that type of responsibility. If the imaginary line falls inside the chin line (or the chin line falls outside of the imaginary line), you are seeing someone who is very capable of handling any authority that is placed on him or her.

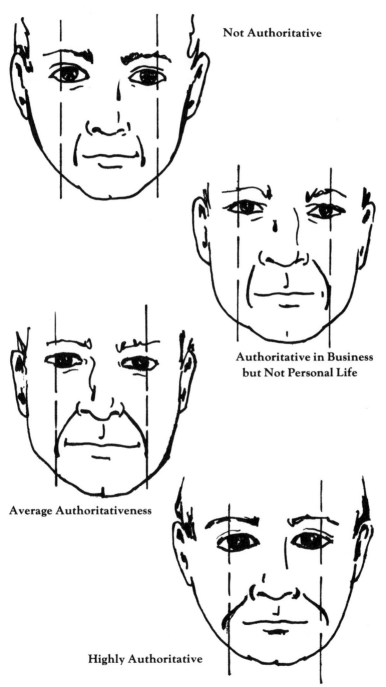

Not Authoritative

Authoritative in Business
but Not Personal Life

Average Authoritativeness

Highly Authoritative

Ear Attachment

How the ears appear to be attached to the head is the trait measurement for the amount of possessiveness in a person. It is one of the most difficult to understand and evaluate, yet it is probably *the* most important trait, next to the eyes. We view this trait from the front, and it often will have left-right differences, indicating possessiveness in one part of a person's life but not in the other. In looking at the face from the front, if the ear appears to be sitting in a cup or indented into the side of the head, then you are seeing one who is *not* possessive. If the ear appears to just attach to the side of the head, not being indented or protruding, then this is considered average. Possessiveness in this manner may be in certain areas.

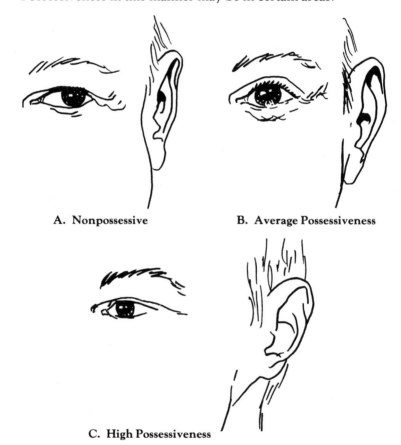

A. Nonpossessive   B. Average Possessiveness

C. High Possessiveness

People with average possessiveness will not be ruled by having to own things, but will usually enjoy the things they own to the fullest and not be prone to giving them up. If the ear appears to sit on a ledge or appears to be an extra part of the head, rather than an integral part of the head, then you are viewing a very possessive person. Other traits will indicate whether a person is possessive of things or people or both. The extremely possessive person does not like to let go of anything, and will often be very jealous in nature. A full understanding of this trait can prevent problems before they are created in a relationship. Determination of home versus business side of the personality is of utmost importance in this trait. Other traits that affect this trait's meaning are nose traits, eye traits, lip traits, and body type.

Ear Placement on the Head

Ear placement is the measurement of how a person looks at life—either idealistically or realistically. It is the basic nature of the personality and has to do with the overall size of the brain cavity. This in no way indicates intelligence levels! The greater the brain cavity, the more idealistic the person. This is measured by viewing the head from the front, and noting where the ear sits on the head. Using the ear canal as the dividing line, measure the amount of head above the canal versus the amount of head below the canal. When you view more head above the canal, you are seeing an idealistic person. When you see more head or face below the canal, then this person looks at life more realistically. The overall measurement is from the base of the chin to the top of the head.

The difference in the two types of people is in their basic nature. The realistic people do not get upset as easily when things go wrong. They feel that tomorrow is another day. The idealistic people, on the other hand, tend to get upset when things don't go just the way they plan. They seem to expect everything to be right. Within our society today, the idealistic people outnumber the realistic people by about two to one.

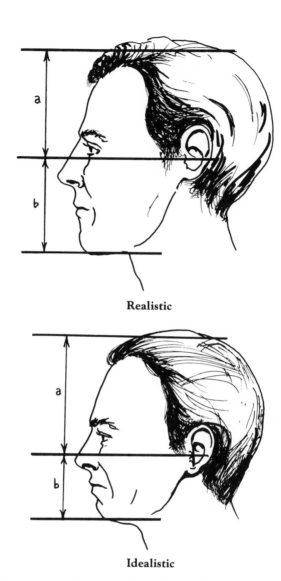

Realistic

Idealistic

Ear Placement—Front to Back on the Head

When the ear sits two-thirds of the way back on the head or more, this is an indication of a forward ego balance. Generally, this is an indication of people who have a high ego, who spend their thought time either in the present or the future. They do not spend much time thinking in the past.

58

They are very aggressive in nature and are the doers of the world. Often they are impatient and less considerate of others. They are too busy thinking toward the future to hold a grudge for any length of time.

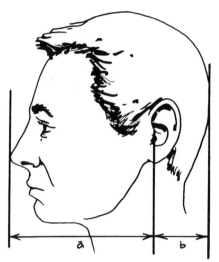

**Ear Two-thirds or More
Back on Head**

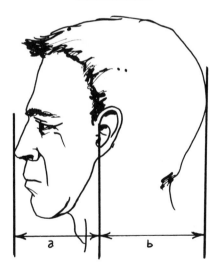

**Ear Less Than Two-thirds
From Back of Head**

Ear Placement Less Than Two-thirds Front to Back

When the ear sits less than two-thirds of the way back on the head, this indicates what is known as a backward ego balance. These people will relate to the present and the past, more so than the future. They will do things based on past experiences and are reluctant to attempt new methods. They are very considerate of others and often appear passive in nature. They have a memory like an elephant and do not forgive easily. They can carry a grudge for years.

Ledge Across the Forehead Above the Eyes

A ledge across the forehead is an indication of people who are very systematic. There will be a right way, a wrong way, and *their* way to do things! They usually have a set system for doing most everything they do, and to relate well to this person you must find out what those systems are and then operate or act within their system. They tend to get extremely upset and agitated when they are forced to operate out of their system, or if their routine is changed.

Forehead Ledge

Half-Moon Protrusions Above the Eyebrows

These people have some similarities to the "ledged-forehead" type of people. They are not quite as systematic but still will notice flaws quickly, and they will be aware of the details of a situation way before others are. They don't like to skip any steps in doing things, and often they will take on other people's problems, whether asked to or not. They are excellent in areas such as proofreading, security checks, or quality-control inspections, because of their ability to notice what is wrong with a situation.

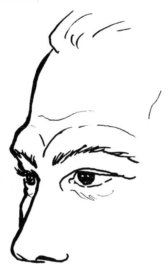

Half-Moon Protrubences

Slant of Forehead

The measurement of how a person thinks, whether it is objective or subjective in nature, is the way in which the forehead slants from just above the eyebrows to the hairline. If the forehead goes straight up, or angles less than 15 degrees, then you have a person who is subjective in nature. If the angle is greater than 15 degrees, then the person is considered to be objective in nature. The difference between the two is as follows: the objective people overcome obstacles as they go; whereas the subjective ones think things out before they start.

We are looking at the front portion of the brain, and this is the thinking portion of the brain. Thus the larger this is (subjective), the more thought will precede action. Those with the crown area of the head that is larger (action portion of the brain) will allow actions to precede thought.

Objective Forehead   **Subjective Forehead**

Crown Dominance Area

The higher the crown area is over the forehead area, the greater the degree of dominance. Unlike authoritativeness, the dominance trait is indicative of those who desire to run the show, and it does not indicate ability to handle others. These people are usually found in front of others, and often it is difficult to communicate with them, because they hear only what they want to hear and like to run things their way. They often appear inconsiderate of others, and occasionally they will try to run your life as well as their own. The trait is measured by comparing the crown of the head to the forehead. The crown area is the action portion of the brain, whereas the forehead area is the thinking portion of the brain.

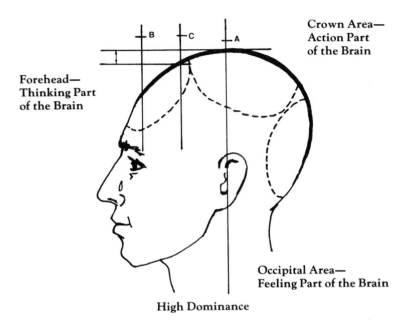

Crown Area—
Action Part
of the Brain

Forehead—
Thinking Part
of the Brain

Occipital Area—
Feeling Part of the Brain

High Dominance

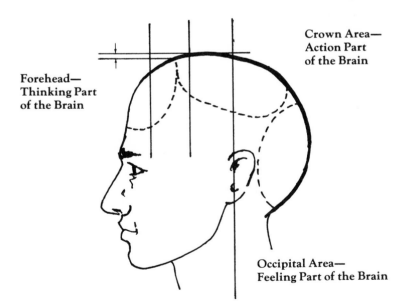

Crown Area—
Action Part
of the Brain

Forehead—
Thinking Part
of the Brain

Occipital Area—
Feeling Part of the Brain

Low Dominance—High Ideas

Square Hairline Around the Forehead

A square hairline indicates the career-minded person. They are very constructive in nature and are good builders both at home and in business. They usually will stair-step their lives in a very orderly fashion.

Square Forehead

Round Forehead at the Hairline

People with a round forehead are the born hosts. They have the ability to flow with almost any situation. They will often find short cuts to getting the job done; however, the end result will be just as complete. They have a natural instinct as a host at parties or functions. They also tend to save everything and could be classified as pack rats.

Round Forehead

Hairline Angles on the Forehead

The way the hairline angles on the forehead toward the top of the head reveals patience and concentration. If the angle is outward, then you are seeing someone with a great deal of patience and an ability for long-range concentration. If the hairline appears to be straight up and down, this would be considered average. If the hairline is angled in, this indicates a lack of patience. This trait is measured on a one-to-ten scale, with one being very impatient and ten, patient.

Great Deal of Patience

Lack of Patience

Average Patience

The Broad Face

The broader the face, the greater the self-confidence. Individuals with very broad faces tend to have a greater degree of self-confidence and will usually tackle most anything with the attitude that they will succeed. They go into a project with this in mind, and thus they are usually successful. The actual measurement is the width of the face versus the height of the face from the chin to the natural turn of the forehead. If the width of the face equals two-thirds the height, the individual will have a better-than-average amount of self-confidence.

Broad Face

The Narrow Face

The narrower the face, the less the self-confidence. This does not mean that people with narrow faces have no self-confidence; rather it pertains to their general outlook. Most people have confidence in their jobs or with the things they feel comfortable with. The lack of self-confidence in this case refers to their outlook at attempting to do things with which they are unfamiliar. They tend to expect the worst, rather than the best. Often these people look at the dark side of things first, then they will look at the bright side, expecting the dark side to show through, and are surprised when the bright side prevails.

Narrow Face

Amount of Upper Lip, Lower Lip, and Chin Protruding From in Front of Eyes

If you drop an imaginary plumb line from between the eyebrows, straight down the face as viewed from the side, then the amount of chin and lips protruding beyond that imaginary line indicates the amount of impetuosity or impulsiveness in a person's nature. This measurement is on a one-to-ten scale, with one being very little and ten being extreme. If only the upper lip is protruding, then this indicates verbal impulsiveness. If the lower lip is protruding, this indicates impulsivity in thought. When the chin is protruding, this is an indication of impulsivity in actions. You will find any combinations of the above, and again, by degree in each of the three areas. (Caution: If you know that the person wears dentures, then this trait must be disregarded.)

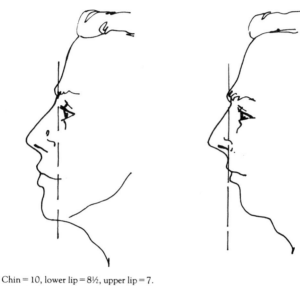

Chin = 10, lower lip = 8½, upper lip = 7.
This indicates greater impulsiveness in
actions than in thoughts or words.

Extreme (10) on the Scale of Impulsiveness

Skin Texture Over Bone Structure

When looking at a person you can determine how the flesh stretches over the bone structure. If it appears to be stretched tight over the bones and looks hard, then you are seeing someone who is tough bodied, and probably tough minded. They will not be as responsive as others and will be prone to be less forgiving. If you see skin that appears loose over the bone structure, then this person is generally more responsive to a given situation. They will generally be gentler and more forgiving.

Thick-skinned People

People with thick skin have a high degree of physical insulation and can stand greater pain than others, because the nerve endings are well protected by the thick skin. These are generally outdoor-type people, and they usually can take more verbal abuse than others. Often they will be less sensitive to others because they do not react to pain or verbal abuse. They will sometimes appear to be abrasive toward others.

Thin-skinned People

The thin-skinned people cannot tolerate a great deal of pain. Their nerve endings are close to the surface of the skin. This makes them much more sensitive; thus they suffer more from both pain and verbal abuse. They get their feelings hurt far faster than the thick-skinned people. If you are around this type of person, be cautious with what you say and be aware of their sensitivity.

Thick Hair Versus Thin Hair

Hair thickness is controlled by the amount of androgen/estrogen balance within the body. The greater the amount of estrogen (female hormone) the greater the amount of hair. The greater the amount of androgen (male hormone) the less the amount of hair. When there is an *imbalance* between the two within the system, it causes either excessive hair or lack of hair, depending on which way the imbalance is—that is, an excessive amount of androgen or a lack of estrogen would create thinning hair.

Coarse Hair Versus Fine Hair

The coarseness or fineness of the hair indicates a way of life. The coarse-haired people generally are doers. They are constantly on the go and will often be found outdoors. They seem to run supercharged all the time. They are accused of having two speeds—faster than a speeding bullet or asleep!

Conversely, fine-textured hair indicates a love of the finer things in life, either esthetic or esoteric. These people like nice things and appreciate quality in most all things. Generally speaking, the finer the hair, the more gentle natured the person.

Beards and Moustaches

Beards and moustaches used to have more significance than they do at present. In the past, a beard meant a person was trying to hide his personality or cover up an insecurity. Often it was used to prove manhood; however, this is no longer the case. In today's society, beards and moustaches are quite common and have no specific meaning by themselves. They do hide some traits and thereby create some problems in reading the facial language. The only meaning that can be applied is to the unkept beard, the one that is allowed to grow wild. This usually indicates a person who is rebelling against the dictates of society.

6
Somatotyping
Physical Body Structures

Somatotyping is a science derived from the ancient Chinese science of physiognomy and deals with the determination of basic general categories of personality traits and patterns in relation to the general appearance of physical body structure.

There are five basic types of physical beings, ranging from super heavies to super lights. These categories have labels or names derived from the genetic embryonic germ layers which gave rise to the cells that developed the physical structure of the body.

The five basic categories are:

Endomorph—super heavies
Mesoendomorph—stout
Mesomorph—body beautiful
Mesoectomorph—slender
Ectomorph—very thin

Each of the five types will be individually examined, and *general* basic characteristics for each will be discussed. Note

71

the use of the term general characteristics. Somatotyping relates to general traits, and often discrepancies occur between personology or face reading and somatotyping. Face reading is specific and more accurate, whereas somatotyping is general and nonspecific, with a good degree of accuracy. Somatotyping is a necessary and excellent point of beginning on which to build from general to specific characteristics. If there is a conflict between the two, always rely on the specific face-reading indicators. Basic motivations are determined primarily through somatotyping.

Through experience, the most successful way to understand others is to understand their basic body type, then look for augmenting facial characteristics, which will indicate that the individual will fit most of the patterns. If the face language defies the body characteristics, be alert for ongoing inner conflicts.

One needs to be careful when reading a person's category, especially when it is a borderline situation. For example, a very heavy mesoendomorph will adopt more characteristics of the endomorph than the mesomorph. Conversely, the meso-endo who has his or her weight under control will adopt more of the characteristics of the mesomorph. An example of this would be Jackie Gleason, a definite mesoendomorph, whose weight fluctuates, and his personality modifies accordingly.

Most experts believe that you are born into a particular category through genetics and you will remain of that type. This may be the case for most people; however, it is not an absolute. There are many cases of people changing their physical structures, and when they change, a corresponding personality change occurs. As an example, observe Frank Sinatra. During his youth he was an ectomorph (skinny). Later, he became a mesoecto (slender), then a mesomorph (well proportioned), and now he is a mesoendomorph (somewhat stout). His face has gone from narrow and angular to round. From information that is common knowledge, his personality has altered correspondingly with his body changes.

With this clarification, we will now proceed to examine each category.

The Endomorph
Basic Motivation—Acceptance

The individual fitting this category is rotund, usually having larger hips than shoulders, short or no neck to speak of, round head, small hands and feet, giving the roly-poly appearance. The most prominent features are the small hands and feet and round head, seemingly out of proportion to the rest of the body. If balding, most endos do so from the back of the head first. Generally, this type individual is very heavy. The chest often has a sunken appearance.

Mother Nature was least kind to this category of people, for they have to carry around excess weight on feet not fully equipped to handle the load. The small chest and lungs are inadequate to provide sufficient air to move about comfortably, and activity often leaves them breathless.

Personality Traits

Endomorphs are food minded and often epicurean in nature. Usually they are excellent cooks of the gourmet variety, and hate to diet. They enjoy home life and can be described as homebodies. Their home is their castle, and they believe in living in it. On visiting endomorphs, do not expect to find a sterile look to their house, as they are adverse to physical work. This does not mean that they are necessarily messy, only that they enjoy their home to the fullest, and it will have that "lived-in" look. Interestingly enough, endos are not big eaters. They will eat more often than others, but not necessarily large quantities. Unfortunately, their metabolism rate is slower than others, and their food is not used up as efficiently as it is by other types. To control their weight, endos will require four or five times as much exercise as other, more-fortunate body types. This makes it tough for them.

These unfortunate heavies have a great need to be accepted by others because of their weight. Therefore, they are very people oriented. Their love of people and their love of life is greater than that of all the others.

Generally, they are very happy, cheerful people, full of enthusiasm, which sometimes gets them in trouble. Because of their desire to be liked by others, they will usually volunteer for anything, resulting in their involvement in more than they can handle, sometimes leaving the false impression that they are incompetent. When dealing with endos, always make sure to allow them adequate time to do what you ask of them.

Being the heavies and not enjoying physical labor, these people try to find an easy way to accomplish their work. This makes them great idea people, far ahead of others in this respect. However don't expect them to figure out the details. That is definitely not their strong suit. They visualize the big, overall picture easily, but the fine details to achieve the goals are beyond their interest.

Endos are excellent entertainers, fond of small talk, and they love to visit. They will go to great extent to create a happy, fun-filled time at parties. Their eternal optimism makes them interesting to be around, and they are the ones who can cheer you up should you be down in the dumps.

Procrastination is a way of life with endos. Their motto should be, "Never do today what you can put off until tomorrow . . . or the next day." They will accept responsibility readily but then not follow through.

Most of these people do not appear to have many clothes, and they usually don't look good in them for two reasons. One is that they are hard to fit, and second, they are more concerned with things other than their looks. Their theme song might be, "Love Me, Love My Weight," or "Why Not Take All of Me?" Their generosity makes them easy prey for unscrupulous people or con artists. They are very sentimental, and this indicates that they will pick up strays, both human and animal. They are real suckers for a sob story, and this often keeps them broke.

The endomorph always wants the seat in the restaurant facing the crowd, for they are very curious and want to see what is happening. They will always be able to recommend a good restaurant.

Their buying patterns generally lean toward the purchase of large items, and they look for benefits rather than details of size, shape, or color.

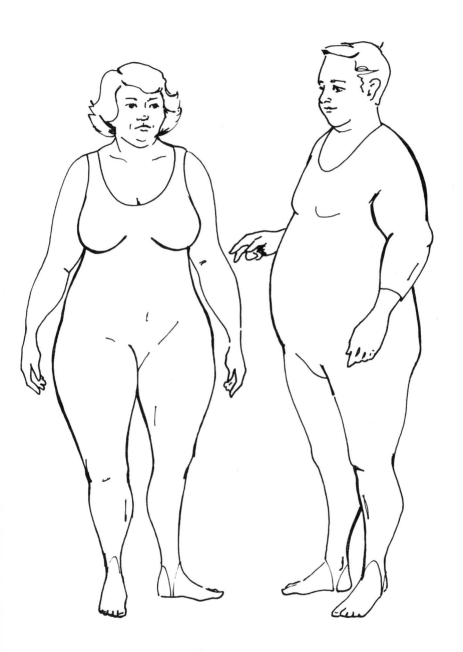

Endomorph

How to Relate to the Endomorph

In an effort to create better harmony with the endo, observe these do's and don'ts.

1. Don't keep them standing on their feet for long periods of time; seat them as soon as possible, facing the crowd.
2. Do ask their opinions, especially about restaurants, recipes, or food-related subjects.
3. Don't discuss business during the main course of the meal. Remember, they make an art of eating, and you should respect this aspect of their nature. Business should be discussed over dessert, because they like to savor sweets to the fullest and like to prolong this enjoyment. Dessert is a particular enjoyment, because it is the last food they will enjoy until the next meal and they realize that it is fattening and that they shouldn't be eating it. Forbidden fruits are always more appealing; therefore, they like prolonging dessert. They treasure this time and will be in high spirits.
4. Do utilize their abilities to relate to other people. This is their best asset.
5. Don't expect them to display great amounts of follow-through on detail. It is not their nature to be concerned with time or details, unless it concerns mealtimes.
6. Don't hire an endomorph for a one-person office. They will go bananas without someone to talk with.
7. Do conduct business with them after mealtime.
8. Don't take them to lunch at a fast-food restaurant. That is almost an insult to them.
9. Do use a lot of small talk and be folksy with them before you get down to business.
10. Don't ask them to spend time in cramped quarters such as compact cars, small rooms, or elevators, because this makes them feel ill at ease.

Remember, the endomorph loves life, people, and food. They are very generous, compassionate people who are not concerned with detail or time, and they are procrastinators personified.

The Mesoendomorph
Basic Motivation—Recognition

Individuals belonging to this group are heavyset, stout-looking people with strong, thick chests and broad shoulders that are wider than the hips. The male appears to be the fatherly type, the female, the motherly type. If balding occurs in the male, it happens at the front and back simultaneously.

Personality Traits

John Shirley, the most knowledgeable man on somatotyping, says of the mesoendomorph, "their theme song is, 'Don't fence me in'." A more descriptive term couldn't be found. It perfectly describes the mesoendomorph personality, for they are truly the freedom lovers, the fun-to-be-around folks. They appear to be always on the go. Their optimism is equivalent to that of the endos, possibly exceeding them. The mesoendo loves to travel. Most of the traveling sales people, both male and female, are mesoendos.

Their aggressiveness is extensive and often gets them into trouble. If ever the phrase "open mouth—insert foot" fit a personality, it would have to be the mesoendo, for often they suffer from extreme cases of the "foot-in-mouth" disease.

These people are the real go-getters, the "make things happen" type of individuals. Take a good look at all the people you consider to be successful, and you will probably find 60 percent or more are mesoendos. This category probably makes more money than all of the others, but that does not necessarily mean that they have money. Money is not their prime motivation. Recognition is! Money serves as the tool to gain recognition; thus mesoendos make their contribution to society by circulating their money. They often talk too much and are generally not the best listeners, because of their aggressive nature.

Many politicians and world leaders belong to this category, because the stouts make things happen. They draw compassion, generosity, and impulsiveness from the endo personality and their drive from the meso personality. Often they are procrastinators, because of their intensity and zest for life.

They especially put off things they don't enjoy doing. They can easily find something to do that has a "higher priority rating" than those things they do not enjoy.

Mesoendos are excellent organizers, good idea people, but like the endomorphs, their attention to details leaves something to be desired. These people need someone to follow them around to take care of details and keep them out of trouble. Once they have laid out the plans for an event, they want to be divorced from it and expect someone else to pick up the ball and run with it. They still want the credit for doing the job, however. Don't expect the stouts to be a whiz at paperwork. These people live life with zeal and gusto.

How to Relate to the Mesoendo

1. Do use reason and logic with them; they will listen if asked to do so.
2. Don't overburden them. They don't like to carry heavy things.
3. Do use their knowledge of eating establishments. They like epicurean foods.
4. Don't force them to sit with their backs to the crowd. Like the endo, they are curious and enjoy the seat facing the action.
5. Do use their ability to communicate with others. This is one of their strengths, if not their best, then close to it.
6. Don't expect them to be good at details, because they favor the endo in this respect.
7. Do use their ability to organize or get a project under way. They are doers and waste little time in starting something.

Remember, the mesoendo's theme song is "Don't Fence Me In," so give them room to operate. They are the fun-loving, freedom-seeking, happy-go-lucky doers and talkers of the world. For them to be happy, they need to be where the action is, and they usually will be found in the thick of it.

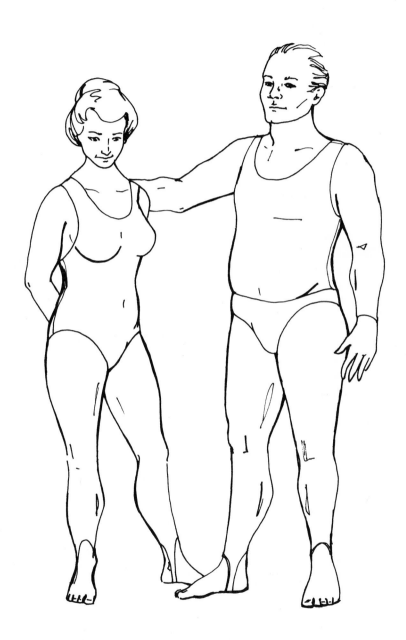

Mesoendomorph

The Mesomorph
Basic Motivation—Variable
Security, Recognition, Power, Money, or People

This category depicts the possessors of the body beautiful. These people are amply endowed with square shoulders that are wider than the hips and strong arms and legs, and they are very athletically inclined. The theme song for this category should be "Don't Mess Around with a Mesomorph," because their predominant characteristic is that *they do not like to lose.*

These are the practical, get-the-job-done type of people. Success is a must with them. They cannot stand to lose, and if they should, a strong tendency to become vindictive is common to most mesomorphs. Never confront this type. One should always flow with them. Mesomorphs are very reluctant to admit to their own mistakes, and for the most part they will usually blame others. They are very practical, materially oriented individuals; therefore, the comforts of the home are valued highly, to the extent that some may be homebodies. These individuals are good organizers and make excellent business people with good follow through. They are dominant, self-centered, competitive, and aggressive. They are exhibitionists, sun worshipers, and spend much time out of doors.

Outward generosity is not overly evident in this group, yet low guilt levels are often displayed. Low guilt levels indicate an attitude of "if someone is going to be stepped on, it will be you before me." The meso often has no compunction about stepping on others to get ahead. There is a stronger influence of vanity experienced in the mesomorph group than any other.

Professional athletes, racecar drivers, football players, and the like are found in this group. They are very dominant, active people. Because of their need to succeed and their aversion to losing, added to low guilt levels, mesomorphs would not hesitate to walk over someone to achieve their goals.

How to Relate to the Mesomorph

1. Do flow with them. Suggest, relate, but never confront them, unless you can do so by making it seem a challenge, and then only if you are sure of yourself. Mesomorphs can be very combative.

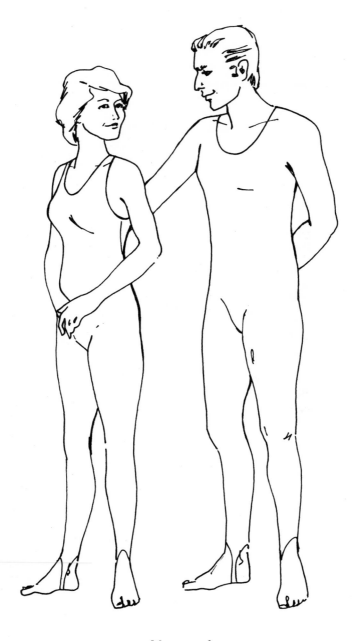

Mesomorph

2. Do respect their time, for they are very conscious of it. Do not waste it.
3. Never take liberties with them, unless they lead you into a situation offering certain liberties.
4. Never complain about aches and pains to a mesomorph, since this has a bad effect on their body consciousness, and they don't like it.

Moderation is always the best approach to a mesomorph. Remember, mesomorphs are very competitive. They are the builders of the world. They don't like to lose and will not admit their mistakes. Their practicality puts them in the forefront, and these are the people who get things done. If you need a job done and done right, with the least amount of expense involved, hire a mesomorph. This category comprises the best business people of all the categories.

Mesoectomorph
Basic Motivation—Security

This category contains two subdivisions of types, both of the linear, slender type. One takes on an ecto influence and one assumes a meso influence.

The ecto influence is demonstrated by people such as doctors and scientists. They are people who are technically oriented, very fastidious, conservative, skeptical, and reserved. They are very conservative with what is theirs, but generous with what is yours. They are very materially oriented, which indicates a lack of willingness to risk themselves, therefore maintaining a protective environment. Often they are insecure and loners, and they are very picky. These people contribute greatly to society.

The meso influence is demonstrated by individuals who are very open, talented, displaying tremendous drive. They are materially oriented, yet they are willing to take calculated risks. These are fun-in-the-sun types—tennis players, perfectionists, hobbyists, and escapists.

Should you be in business, particularly sales, and a mesoectomorph comes in, you might as well send him to competitors. He will waste your time on minute details, because of

Mesoectomorph

his picky nature, and he will rarely buy, preferring probably to purchase from mail order. The mesoectos found in politics are the very conservative individuals who are very conservative with what is theirs and very generous with what is yours. They are the ones wanting change for the sake of change. Mesoectos are very reserved and will not be open with you easily, but when they are, they will be open all the way.

The mesoecto has the ability to see and note the details. They make excellent quality-control inspectors or proof-readers. Their ability to see and define faults makes them very valuable assets in many businesses. Too often they take this talent home with them and when this happens, what is an asset at work becomes intolerable criticism at home. Their concern with perfection and details is quickly seen in their homes, for generally nothing is out of place, and everything has its place.

If you have mesoecto friends, they will be quick to notice any changes in you and can be very complimentary, especially when the changes made (such as weight loss) are more in tune with their thinking.

These people are very hard workers. They are of the 8-to-5 variety, generally, and expect to be well compensated for it. They will usually give you an honest day's work for an honest day's pay.

How to Relate to the Mesoecto

1. Don't expect them to take risks. They are not risk prone. If they work for you, don't force them to operate on a commission basis, for they need the security of knowing where their next paycheck is coming from.
2. Don't force the mesoecto who leans toward the ecto side to mix well in a crowd of people. They do not like to be put into a crowd, preferring to be observers.
3. Do use their talents to analyze a situation. Remember, they are very good at finding the details.
4. Do value their opinions and judgment on values. They will usually research items well before making a purchase, and they will almost always know where the best price can be found.

5. Don't threaten the mesoecto, because this will often cause them to do unusual things. They do not react as the other categories do when placed in jeopardy.
6. Do use their abilities and talents. This category produces many extremely talented people in many different fields.
7. Do not expect them to be generous with what is theirs, as they find security in owning things.

In dealing with a mesoecto or ectomorph in business, use the mild-mannered, factual approach. Do not sell the sizzle. Forget your interest and concentrate on theirs. Never try to force fast decisions on them; it is not their nature. They are the proverbial "tire kickers."

Ectomorphs
Basic Motivation—Security,
Often Achieved Through Knowledge

Those belonging to the ectomorph group are the thin, artistic-looking individuals, with long, slender hands and feet. They are very shy, gentle, reserved, indoor thinking types who prefer to be alone in a protected environment. These people are security-motivated perfectionists, and they can be boring. They make excellent teachers, professors, scientists, and doctors.

These are the brain-oriented people—people who contribute greatly to our society. This type is very gentle in nature, and when dealing with one you never want to place them in a crowd or harsh physical contact surroundings. Even in their choice of art, they will choose the more-subdued, subtle works of art, compared with the mesoendos, who will pick very bright types of art.

The ectos do well in sports that do not involve direct physical contact with others. Such sports as table tennis, bowling, or even tennis are good examples. Their long arms and legs become an asset in these sports. The ecto is not risk prone, and you will rarely find an ectomorph in a job situation that requires working on a commission for pay. They prefer a salaried position in which they know what income they have coming in.

Often their motivation is knowledge. They love to learn and usually are avid readers. They have a great deal to offer our society, in that as the thinkers, these people really can come up with ideas. Their lack of physical stamina and their increased mental activity makes them excellent inventors of labor-saving devices. If you need to do something with less effort, ask an ecto. They can figure out the easiest, least-physical way to get the job done.

When you are around an ecto, you need to think fast on your feet. Remember, they are brain oriented and often will be way ahead of you in their thought process. This sometimes works to their disadvantage, in that others often misunderstand them, especially when they think faster than they speak.

In dealing with ectomorphs, remember to use the same tactics as in dealing with the mesoectomorphs, who derive their traits from this ecto influence. Treat them gently, with respect, and expect them to be detail oriented.

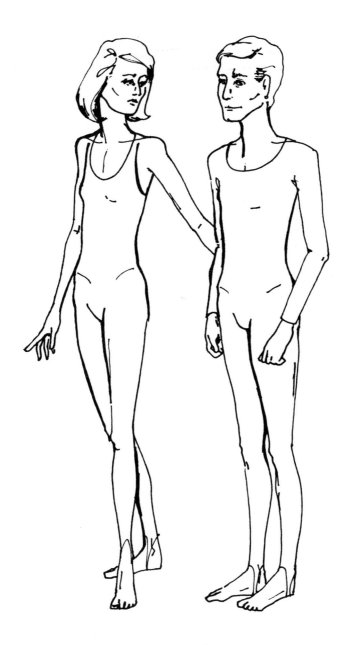

Ectomorph

7
Gestures
Body Language

Hand Talking

Almost all of us use our hands in talking. If the hands are palm up and moving toward the body, this is an indication of sincerity and integrity. If they are palm down and moving away from the body, this indicates a lack of sincerity. If this is coupled with jerky motions, then the person may not be telling the truth. The downward, away-from-the-body motion is saying, "Away. No. I don't believe it. Keep it away from me." If a person uses his or her hands to point at you, he or she is emphasizing a point or trying to dominate you by threats or power.

Arms and/or Legs Crossed

It has generally been thought that when people have their arms or legs crossed they are acting closed or defensive. This is *not* always the case. In fact, more often this is now considered a relaxation pose. The key to determining the difference is in

89

what the rest of the body is doing. If the arms are crossed, the hands are gripping the forearms, and the knuckles are white with tension, then *yes*, that person is defensive. Also, if the legs are crossed and appear tense, that action is considered closed or defensive. Add to either or both of these the down-turned head, and maybe a scowl on the face, and this person isn't even listening. Conversely, if there is no sign of tension and no scowl, then this just becomes a relaxed position.

Handshake

The handshake will give you a measure of a person's confidence, especially in men. The stronger the grip, the greater the level of confidence. Although women do not ordinarily shake hands the way men do, when they do grasp even your fingers, this still indicates their degree of confidence. The exception to this is when a woman offers her hand palm down as though it were meant to be kissed. This is a mark of femininity or graciousness.

Preening Gestures

Preening gestures are numerous and involve those movements designed to make us feel better, such as patting our hair in place, tucking in a shirt, smoothing a skirt, or picking imaginary lint off our clothes. This is saying, "I want to make a good impression."

Dominant Stance Versus the Slouch

The dominant or military stance or walk indicates confidence. The slouch, or drooped-shoulder walk, is an indication of lack of confidence. The dominant, straightforward walk indicates an expectation of positive happenings, whereas the drooped-shoulder walk indicates an expectancy of negative things. These people feel "stepped on" and usually are.

Constant Movement

The people who just can't seem to sit still are telling you that they are: (1) nervous, or have an excess amount of energy

(2) not interested in what is happening around them. They may also be concerned about something else at that time. In either case, you do not have their full attention.

Hand Movements

The hand in front of the mouth indicates a desire to interrupt and add to the conversation. People who keep their hands in front of their mouths while speaking lack confidence in what they are saying, or they lack confidence in themselves. The hands and fingers entwined, especially while seated, indicates thought process at work.

When a person is listening to another and is scratching an ear òr ear lobe, it indicates that he or she is not sure of what is being said. It is best to repeat yourself if you see this. Scratching the head also indicates an unsureness, as if saying, "I'm not quite certain I understand."

Hands in Pocket—Fiddling with Loose Coins

When a man has his hands playing with the loose change in his pocket, regardless of whether he is talking or listening, this is an indication of concern for money. People who do this are either thinking about money or are in a selling situation in which they are concerned with the amount or the cost.

Nervous Energy

Nervous energy is often a sign of lack of concentration or attention. When people constantly tap their fingers or shake their legs, or show other nervous-energy habits, it usually indicates that they are thinking of something or someone else. Occasionally it can indicate fear, when undergoing an interview, taking an exam, or in a similar situation.

8

The Meaning of Clothes and Style

Soft Pastel Colors

Basically, soft pastels, solid in color, are an indication of the need for gentleness. The person wearing this type of clothing is often nonaggressive in nature and seeks harmony in his or her life.

Bright, Sharp Colors

Lively patterns that stand out in clothing and bright, sharp colors indicate outgoing, aggressive people who like to consider themselves as different from the ordinary. They tend to be extroverted in nature, or they have the desire to be extroverted. Generally, the more outlandish the outfit, the more individualistic the person. You will rarely see a person dressed in bright colors who is "down" or moody while wearing these colors. Happiness in attitude goes hand in hand with bright colors.

The Efficient Business Look

The person who wears relatively basic, conservative busi-ness-type clothes is trying to create that impression. These people want to be considered good business people. When you see the basic business suit or dress, augmented by extreme contrast in accessories, such as navy blue with a bright red tie, this is telling you that here is a person who has a sense of business, with a flair for challenge or a willingness to take a chance. If the accessories match the clothes or are not in sharp contrast, then this will tell you that that person goes by the rules and follows the standard procedures.

Jewelry

An excessive amount of jewelry is an indication of possess-iveness of material things and usually means the person measures success by material gains. When you see a person with only one or two pieces of high-quality jewelry, then you are a witness to someone who enjoys the finer things in life. It indicates a love of quality rather than quantity. A complete lack of jewelry indicates a person who is not motivated by money at all. This type of person generally does not relate to worldly goods, but usually relates to the esthetic or esoteric values in life.

Unbuttoned Blouses or Shirts

Women who wear blouses or men who wear shirts with two or three buttons unbuttoned are indicating a need for sexual attention of one kind or another. The need may be for attention only rather than an actual desire for sexual contact. Genuine compliments will go a long way in creating a good relationship with these people, for they are saying non-verbally, "Wake up and notice me!"

Black and Red Colors

Black and red are stronger indicators of mood than any other colors. When you see basic black (except for formal wear) on a person, it can have one of two meanings. First, it can indicate a negative mood or represent a gloomy feeling. Second, and more frequently the case, black is often worn as a color of power. The person who is trying to communicate a need for control over others will often wear a great deal of black. It is also considered an occult color, again denoting power.

Red, on the other hand, is tied into sensuality. Depending on the shade of red and the style of the clothes, this color is attempting to say sexy or seductive. Most people choose their clothes oblivious to the hidden meanings they are attempting to express. Observation of what people wear can be a real key to understanding basic motivations in personalities.

9

Basic Motivation

The motives that guide our actions are much like the pipes of an organ, in that they are often hidden from view. Understanding what motivates us is an important part of self-awareness, and it is a key to understanding the actions of others. Knowing what prompts people to do what they do is basic to understanding how to relate to them. Understanding our own motivation is the first step in self-awareness and self-improvement.

There are certain basic motivation factors common to all in various degrees. These factors may be numbered and classified differently, according to the various psychologists who have documented them. However, there are certain basic motivational factors we may examine that pertain to the average person. They are fundamental.

Most of us at one time or another are motivated by recognition and the desire to be accepted by others. Recognition and acceptance by others are a part of our basic desires for which we all strive, some more so than others. This factor relates to our need for security, both physically and psycho-logically. The sense of security is a strong motivation factor that may manifest as a need for material comforts or as a need to belong, to be wanted, to be worthwhile. Survival instincts are the parent of security motivation. It is the strongest inherent basic need. To live, to exist, to be secure, to be happy . . . these are the offspring of survival motivation. The corresponding emotions to these motivation factors are: de-sire, faith, hope, love, enthusiasm, romance, and sex. The opposing fears are: poverty, criticism, ill health, loss of love, old age, and death.

Life is a struggle wherein we attempt to balance these positive and negative forces to achieve harmony, thus fulfill-ing our basic needs to be secure and loved, to be accepted, and to be sound in physical and mental health. Understanding our motivations, emotions, and fears will aid us in developing a positive mental attitude and the self-discipline necessary to attain these goals. Motivational factors are not always constant throughout life. They may adjust to physical and mental growth, varying with time periods. Changes in attitude and needs may affect changes in motivation. The adolescent will be motivated differently from the adult, the single person differently from the married one, and the divorced person differently than either of the others.

It is appropriate at this point to review the basic motiva-tions applicable to the somatotypes.

Endomorphs

Their basic motivation is acceptance. The heavy-sets need to be wanted and needed because of their size and weight. Recognition for the endomorph will take the form of the need to be accepted by others; therefore, they are people oriented, desiring to be needed and approved by others. Their security is gained by the degree to which they are recognized and accepted for what they are. Endomorphs judge success on the basis of the number of people who do accept them as they are and for what they are. This is general, and other basic motivational factors may also enter into the total motivational picture. Materialistic recognition is the exception with the endomorph, not the rule. Home usually equals security to these people, and their home is their castle. They find the most comfort there. This is usually the only materialistic need they express, and it is basically for comfort, not for status.

Mesoendomorphs

The stouts are recognition motivated. The need for people to know who they are and what they are is essential to the mesoendomorphs. Often they are materialistic and judge success by their possessions. To this type, recognition may take on the form of status symbols and materialism or people-oriented recognition. These are active, fun-loving, outdoor types. Security motivation is sometimes evident in the mesoendomorphs, but not as a rule. Sometimes the mesoendos will display the need to control, and power becomes a motivation factor.

Mesomorphs

Mesomorphs are more difficult to determine as to motivation. Basically, their need is for security. This can manifest itself in materialism, recognition, and/or power. Generally, this type judges success by material possessions. Whenever you find a mesomorph who is people oriented, desiring to help others, you have found a super, super human being. These are the practical ones who know the value of a dollar and how to keep it, but when they become people oriented, they want to share and do for others. They have the stamina, the knowledge, and the ability to do much for others what they have done for themselves.

Mesoectomorphs

The mesoectos are definitely security motivated. This manifests from the mesomorphic side in the form of recognition. The meso influence, when dominant, gives rise to a fun-loving, outgoing individual who judges success by material things, yet relates extremely well with people.

The mesoecto with a strong ecto influence will seek security from knowledge and through the use of information will seek material things that maintain a protective environment. Primarily, security is derived from their knowledge. These types would much prefer a PhD after their names than money in the bank. Success is judged by material things, but not to the extent of the other types.

Ectomorphs

The basic motivation of the ectomorphs is the need for security. These people need the influence of salaried jobs and secure home lives. They rarely will succeed in commission-type work and will generally choose work that does not involve mixing with a lot of people. They work well in one person offices. Knowledge also provides security to the ectomorph; thus we find a great many PhD's in this category.

Somatotyping, as we have pointed out earlier, is general and less specific than face language. By using it as a starting point of reference and tying it into nonverbal communication, one can develop a keen understanding of human nature. To illustrate, imagine an endomorph who is outgoing, folksy, and fun to be around and who needs to be recognized by other people. Add to this the hook nose, thin lips, analytical or critical eyes, and you know that you are not dealing with a basic endomorph—one who is not people motivated—but rather one who is motivated by material things. In this case the augmenting nonverbal traits indicate a deviation from the purely endomorphic traits. Remember that the nonverbal traits are more accurate than the general somatotypes and that the combination of both gives a more-complete, specific, and accurate analysis of the personality.

Another example would be the mesomorph who has very thick lips, straight nose, and large eyes. The basic motivation is security, based on the meso influence. Add to these traits a lot of rhetoric lines, humor lines and expression lines, such as might be found on a teacher, and security in this hypothetical case will probably be expressed by the need for recognition as a secondary motivator. Success would be judged by material things accumulated. The need to be recognized for oneself would be satisfied by teaching and relating to people. This person would judge success by his or her standard of living.

For comparison, look at another mesomorph who is a politician. At once you would know that recognition is a prime motivator. Security for this one would take on another form. Material motivation may still be a factor, but basic security would be expressed by recognition. In this case, power motivation may be a factor. Some politicians feel the need to control or to dominate, and the desire to gain power recognition becomes a driving force. If the eyes are small in this type individual, then the power motivation is known to be a factor. The small, nonemotional eye indicates a low guilt level and concern with self. The defiant chin, the wedge-shaped, stubborn, angular chin, is another augmenting trait. For comparison, consider the mesoendo who is recognition motivated and add to this good self-expression lines, good humor lines, large eyes, and a rounder or more square chin, and say that this person is a public speaker. Recognition would still be the motivational factor, but it would take the form of personal recognition by other people. This person wants to be liked by people. This type would be easygoing, friendly, always in the forefront, seeking acceptance and good will from others. Material things may not be a goal for this type; however, it might be the way to measure success.

Here it becomes evident that somatotypes with the same basic motivation may differ in manifestation according to the augmenting traits. The entire composite structure of non-verbal traits and somatotyping characteristics must be viewed from an individual perspective, keeping in mind the augmenting traits.

Using Body Talk in Man-Woman Relationships

10
Understanding the Keys to Personality Traits

Communication

To communicate means to impart or convey a message from one person to another in such a way as to make the meaning of the message understood.

Messages may be conveyed in written, verbal, or electronic forms, but more importantly, many messages may be conveyed nonverbally. More often than not, there is a great deal more expressed nonverbally than verbally. Understanding face language will provide the key to a better and more complete understanding of the verbal messages conveyed through a better knowledge of what is being said nonverbally.

Understanding the personality traits reflected by the facial indicators of face language will give a keener insight into the nature of the perspective from which an individual will examine the message you are trying to communicate. Each of us must form our opinion on the basis of inferences made from our personal perspective, drawing from past experiences, intelligence, and personality. Everything we perceive, each message we receive, is shaded by our concept of what is being communicated, drawn from conclusions based on our understanding from our personal viewpoint or perspective.

For example, if we say the word "blue," each of us will call to mind the color blue. But, will each of us have in mind the same shade? The answer is no! If we held up a navy blue tie and said the word "blue," then each of us would understand the meaning of the word blue in this instance. A thing or phrase does not have the same meaning to each of us until we view the object from the same perspective. What we might call a desk in America might be called a table in France. The object is the same, but the meaning of the descriptive words is different. Understanding what is meant by the language depends on the perspective. To make ourselves understood, therefore, we must communicate from the proper perspective in a manner that conveys the same thought wherever we are.

Human relations are often strained by the lack of communication because of the inability to relate to one another and to convey the meaning of thoughts in a manner readily understood. In relationships of mates, lovers, and friends, the breakdown of communication lies in the lack of understanding of basic personality differences and the inability to relate on a one-to-one basis. Often we try to communicate, but we find that what we are trying to say is not understood. Failure to make ourselves understood often leads to frustration, aggression, and hostility. The more we are misunderstood, the stronger the tendency to become reticent, until we finally stop trying to communicate.

When communication between two people stops, the relationship is doomed to failure unless the situation is corrected. Why do we fail to communicate? Very often we fail to see things from the perspective of another person. The more information we have about the personality traits of the person we want to communicate with, the more easily we can predict the reaction one is most likely to receive in a given situation. The more we understand about the personality, the easier it is to place ourselves in the other person's place and visualize things from that perspective. With greater knowledge of the other person's viewpoint, we can relate more meaningfully and make ourselves more easily understood. In nonverbal communication or face language, understanding some of the keys to personality traits will assist us in understanding what is being said. Compatible types communicate more easily; however, when there are differences in personalities, understanding the differences will enable us to relate better.

For example, let us consider the case of a person who has the flat eyebrow, indicating the need and desire for harmony in a relationship, and a person who has the highly arched eyebrow, indicating the very dramatic person. Usually the person with the flat eyebrow, when speaking, comes directly to the point, succinctly, without embellishments. The person with the highly arched eyebrow usually embellishes the conversation with many adjectives because of the very dramatic outlook on life so typical of this type. This type person may get so carried away with dramatizing the conversation that the point may become lost to the more concise flat-eyebrowed person. The dramatic person sees life from a broader perspective, entirely different from the flat-eyebrowed person, and the basic differences may lead to misunderstanding of the true meaning of what is being said.

It is important to take into consideration the combinations of face language indicators that augment this situation. The height of the eyebrow over the eye indicates aloofness. If the eyebrow is low over the eye, this indicates the friendly, down-to-earth type. The higher the eyebrow sits over the eye, the more reserved the person will be. This type requires respect and is very formal. It is difficult for this type to make and accept friends, but once accepted as a friend, it will be a lasting relationship. Very often this type will come in contact with someone with eyebrows close to the eyes, then wonder why the association does not work. Basically, the one with eyebrows high over the eyes is very reserved and has a fear of rejection, which in this case means that this person does not want to share any thoughts, because of the fear of rejection or a fear that others will not want to hear what he or she might say. This fear may be present in many, but it is held more in check by those who have eyebrows close to the eyes. The low-eyebrowed person, on finding out about this reservation, will feel deceived, not realizing that the other person withheld from a fear of rejection, not from a lack of wanting to share. It is not difficult to see the potential conflicts arising from the basic differences of these two types.

Should you be a person with the high eyebrow, try to look at every situation from the other person's viewpoint, looking at it objectively. From this perspective you will probably find that what you hesitate to do or share with others relates to your judgment of what is good or bad and is based on a fear of criticism by others.

The purpose of understanding face language is to provide a practical means by which one may better know how to relate to others in daily personal relationships. It is best to ascertain, at the beginning of an association, those facial indicators that will most affect the relationship. By recognizing the important personality traits, one may know how to relate better to each individual. The more we understand about the person, the more intelligently we can deal with the person. Therefore, it is best to note the more obvious traits, especially those that indicate how a person tends to look at life and the attitude that person takes toward how to live. The high or low position of the eyebrow is an important indicator of the total outlook on life a person takes.

For consideration next will be the cheekbones. The high cheekbones indicate an adventurous attitude toward life. This attitude is expressed by the desire for adventure in one's life. The desire may be expressed in action or deeds, or it may be expressed in mental attitude and thought. The higher the cheekbone, the higher the desire for adventure. Here again we can see that this type person married to one who is not adventurous would possibly face conflicts. The adventurous person would always want to go places and do and see different things. The nonadventuresome nature would much prefer to stay at home.

The adventurous person may tend to get bored with the relationship, and often this type person might begin to feel that the partner does not want to be with him or her, when in fact it is nothing more than a difference in outlook. If this situation is not recognized and dealt with in an intelligent manner, irreparable harm to the relationship may result. Recognizing and knowing how to cope with such differences is the key to improving personal relationships and therein lies the true value of face language.

Next, we will examine the differences between the emotional person (as determined by the large eyes) and the nonemotional or small-eyed individual. By emotional we do not just mean the person who cries at sad movies. Rather, the type of reaction one might take to any given situation is more indicative of emotionalism. Emotion is an automatic reaction to a situation expressed with great feeling, and this is as much an attitude toward life as it is an expression of emotions.

The highly emotional person is easily hurt, since everything is taken in a personal way. If someone used verbal abuse, the emotional person would accept this personally and feel hurt. Verbal abuse will not run off the emotional person's back like water off a duck. It sticks like glue.

Visualize, if you will, a person with large emotional eyes married to a person with small, nonemotional eyes. The one with small irises may have feelings just as strong as the person with large emotional eyes, but the difference is that the small-eyed person doesn't show emotion but rather holds it in. The difference is in *response* to a situation. The large-eyed person reacts emotionally, and the small-eyed person reacts in a nonemotional manner, even though both may have equally strong feelings. The small-eyed person can hide emotions extremely well, and the large-eyed person cannot. Realizing this, it is easy to understand how a union of two such opposite types could come to the point that the emotional one would think "You do not understand my feelings."

"I don't understand you, you don't know how I feel." The reason for this type of thinking becomes apparent when the differences in basic personality traits are understood. The conflict arises from a difference in reactions to the same situation expressed in opposite ways. In reality, the small-eyed person does understand, but does not show it through emotions. Therefore, if placed in a situation such as this, the small-eyed person would benefit by learning to be more understanding and more giving to the more-emotional mate. Likewise, the more-emotional person would do well to realize a less-emotional response does not mean that there is a lack of feeling or a lack of caring, but rather a difference in natures. Understanding and relating to the other person's feelings is always the key to better relationships.

The lips are the indicators of generosity. The thicker the lips, the greater the degree of generosity. Generosity implies not only money, but also time and deeds. Thick upper lips indicate verbal generosity. This type likes to share things verbally. Thick lower lips indicate generosity in action and deeds. The thick lower lips belong to automatic givers, those who readily give of themselves. Imagine a realtionship involving a person with very thin lips and a person with very thick lips. The thin-lipped person would tend to resent the thick-lipped person's generosity to others and would think "Hey! Do it for me, not for everyone else."

Jealousy is very often a by-product of this type of situation. It is not difficult to envision the potential for conflict in a relationship of this type. Understanding this potential and adjusting to the differences will be of great value. If you are an overly generous person and your mate or friend is not, restraint might be in order. At least, devoting more time and attention to your mate could be helpful. Generosity is a very noble trait, but beware of making a vice of a virtue. Moderation in all things is a very good rule to follow. Here again, understanding and accepting and relating to basic differences is the key to better relationships. The thin-lipped person would do well to recognize and accept the fact that the thick-lipped person is generous by nature and to accept him or her is to accept and expect that characteristic.

Business acumen, sense of value, and sense of money are indicated by the shape of the nose. The hook nose is the sign of good business people who know the value of the dollar and who are capable of making money. They are usually price oriented and expect to be paid for what they do. When you see a person with this type nose and a combination of the thick generous lips of the automatic giver, generosity will most probably be expressed at home or with friends or relatives. This type person will tend to be conservative with money except with family, where they will be quite generous.

The helper nose or the up-turned nose belongs to the person who likes to be helpful. These people give of themselves, and money is not a primary motivation. Imagine the disasterous situation of a relationship between a person with a hook nose and thin lips and a person having the up-turned nose and thick lips. The hook nose and thin lips would indicate a not-overly-generous person who is very conservative with money, and the thick lips and up-turned nose of the other person would indicate an automatic giver, generous with time and money, compounded with the helpful nature of the willing helper—an almost impossible combination. Should two people such as these get together, most certainly there would be conflicts and arguments over money. This relationship could be doomed from the start. One would be concerned with making and holding on to money, and the other would tend to give everything away. This situation would require a tremendous amount of love and understanding for the relationship to survive. Being aware of the factors that create the potential for conflict such as this should be very helpful in preventing problems and in solving existing difficulties.

Traits to look for in the choice of our mates, lovers, and friends that indicate qualities inherently helpful in developing a smooth and happy relationship are the combinations of traits which show a high degree of sympathy. These indicators are the combinations of emotionality, helpfulness, and generosity. The large eyes, up-turned nose, thick lips, and eyebrows close to the eyes are the traits indicating these qualities. Combinations of these traits belong to the person who is friendly, sympathetic, open-minded, generous, and helpful in nature. Conversely, the small-eyed, hooked-nose, thin-lipped person would be skeptical, nonemotional, conservative, and not openly generous or understanding. A union of two people with these contrasting traits would be a very difficult relationship, one not likely to thrive.

Communication does not just mean the ability to converse well. Obviously, there is much more involved than just the use of words. Attunement and relating to the other person is an important aspect of conveying messages. Face language is an excellent means by which this attunement may be achieved. A gentle, reassuring touch of the hand at the right moment may well express more than any words for those who are in tune with each other. What we communicate nonverbally is just as meaningful and important as anything that we may verbally communicate, and often it has more impact. Recognizing the factors that communicate on a nonverbal basis and understanding how to relate to these factors are very important parts of the communicative process.

The position of the eyebrow over the eye, the shape of the eyebrow, the size of the iris of the eye, the shape of the nose, the shape of the lips, and the following two other traits come into play as major factors in the nonverbal communication process. The distance from the upper contour of the lip to the base of the nose indicates the degree of vanity. The shape of the chin indicates the degree of stubbornness. To be compatible, it is best to find someone who is in the same boat as you are. The role vanity plays will illustrate what might happen when two people of opposite traits enter into a relationship.

Vanity usually refers to people who like to dress well, look neat, and keep their bodies in good condition. These people expect others to do the same. If you are not a vain person, not overly concerned with your appearance, there is a possibility that your lack of concern in this regard would tend to irritate the vainer person.

Being vain is not in itself a negative quality. Indeed, it is important to have a good self-image. The overemphasis of an extremely vain person can cause problems when involved in a relationship with someone who is not. The vain person will tend to criticize the other by saying, "Why don't you take better care of yourself? Why don't you want to look better?" Also, the vain person may be more extravagant in spending money for clothes, cosmetics, hairstyles, and the like. The vain person will most likely be more interested in physical fitness than the one who is not. This could lead to disharmony in the choice of recreations such as sports activities not mutually shared. Here again, the choice of combination of personality types most nearly alike will usually be the best. The more differences in personality traits involved in a relationship, the more need for understanding and a conscious effort to compensate for the differences. Love and understanding and a willingness to accept people as they are will overcome any differences, but it is more difficult.

Opposites do seem to attract, yet sometimes they repel like magnets placed together at the wrong poles. Sometimes a person will need opposite traits in a partner to give balance and compensate for deficiencies in his or her own personality. It is the extremes and excesses not understood and dealt with that cause the problems.

The last indicator in this area of face language is the shape of the chin. The greater the degree to which the chin is wedge shaped and pointing downward, the greater the degree of stubbornness. The person with the squarer-shaped or softer-shaped chin that is more rounded will be more flexible. Once again, imagine two people who are both extremely stubborn in nature living together. Neither will give in or admit to mistakes. Each thinks he or she is right in any given situation. Both are assured in their own minds that theirs is the only way to do things. In this particular trait you may not want to look for opposites, but rather, it is one that you will need to understand. Accept the fact that you are stubborn and that you are determined to do things in your own way, but also, accept the right of your mate or friend to do the same. Being aware of the nonverbal communicators helps to create a smoother and more pleasant life-style in our daily relationships.

For the sake of good communication, take a close look at yourself in the mirror and determine your strengths and weaknesses using the guidelines in the book. Evaluate your personality and accept the things that are a part of your nature. Should you desire to alter some aspect of these traits, be aware of that. Then look for similar qualities in the person you want to relate to. Accept and understand the qualities that you find in others, and relate to what you learn from the nonverbal communicators in dealing with them. If you are married to someone and only now realize certain differences and you want to restore some of that romantic spark and revitalize your relationship, face language can help. It has been said that marriage is the fastest way to break up a good romance. All too often this is true, but it need not be so. The following example will illustrate.

Let us say that you are a flat-eyebrowed mesomorph in business, with a straight nose, average eyes, and average thickness of lips. You are then known to be a doer, a very objective person who is out to conquer the world. You are married to a person with extremely high cheekbones, arched eyebrows, large eyes, a turned-up nose, and thick lips. You are married to an ideal romanticist. This is a person who wants and expects constant change, constant romance, and much attention. This is the type of person you need to surprise every so often. Unexpected gifts, flowers, or romantic dinners in a quiet atmospheric restaurant will do wonders to maintain or restore that element of magic to a tired marriage. After all, you did these things when you were dating, why not do them now? Very often this will spark a new relationship in a marriage that has become worn.

This is the most common situation found in counseling married couples whose marriage, while not on the rocks, has lost that "zing," and neither knows why. Pretend you are once again dating your mate and do all those little thoughtful things you did to impress each other when you were dating. It worked once; it will work again. Marriages such as this often get in trouble because the parties no longer relate to each other as they once did. Both have become set in their own way according to the traits indicated by their face language. At this point they think in terms of "Well, she should understand better," or "He should know that this is the way I am."

Look for nonverbal communications. They can tell you a great deal, and understanding them will point to a solution to problems. People can, after understanding the art of Body Talk, take the traits they disliked and work on them, ultimately being able to change them and by so doing, improve their marriage.

Conversation is the most common form of communication. Good company and good conversation are the ingredients that give the hope of joy in human relations. Knowing when and how to be a good listener is a valid part of the art of conversation. Other ingredients that make an art of conversation are: first, the ingredient of truth; next, good sense; third, good humor; fourth, wit; fifth (and most important) communication. Conversation without the communication of thoughts, concepts, and ideas being conveyed to the listener is nothing more than modulations of sound in thin air.

Nonverbal communication is the key to the vault containing the riches that make conversation a true and meaningful communicative experience.

11
Possessiveness Indicators

The desire to own or possess either material things or people is a psychological force very prevalent in our society, deeply instilled in our thoughts and deeds. We have all been so programmed by the materialistic nature of our complex, industrial-scientific progress that, unfortunately, we have come to measure a person's worth by the amount of material possessions and wealth accumulated. Many people carry this psychological desire to own or possess to the extreme in their personal relationships, desiring to own or possess people just as they would material things, thus giving rise to the personality trait of possessiveness in regards to mates, lovers, and friends.

What fascination and charm there is to be found in the phrases "one's own," "it is mine," "I own it," "you are mine," "you belong to me." Yes, there is special attraction and satisfaction to all of us in varying degrees found in the use of these phrases. In the pursuit of all worldly things, people act

117

with great eagerness and intention of mind, yet they find not half the pleasure in the actual possession as in the expectation. Shakespeare so aptly wrote, "It so falls out that what we have, we prize not to the worth whiles we enjoy it, but being lacked and lost, why then we rack the value; then we find the virtue that possession would not show us whiles it was ours."

Possessions can be either good or bad, depending on our use of them. Without proper usage, wealth, power, friends, servants, or material things do little else but make our lives more unhappy. Attainment is often followed by neglect, and possession by disgust. A very wise Brahman verse states, "Possess nothing, that nothing may possess thee."

The foregoing prologue is not an attempt to moralize; it is an attempt to emphasize the nature and extent to which the desire to possess or own material things and/or people influences our daily lives. Also, it points out that the personality trait of extreme possessiveness carries with it the seeds of discord, disharmony, dissention, and despair. When the seeds are nurtured and mature, the fruits are very bitter. More simply, to illustrate the nature of possessiveness, imagine you have a wet bar of soap in your hand and you begin to squeeze the soap. The harder you squeeze, the more difficult it is to hold the bar, until finally the pressure of your grip will force the soap to fly out of your hand. Such is the nature of extreme possessiveness. The harder you try to hold onto what you desire to possess, the more elusive and difficult to hold it will become. It is almost as though we try to smother that which we prize the most. This is not to say that owning things is wrong; on the contrary, it is a fact of life and a must to survival, an accumulation of rewards in exchange for our efforts. It is when these rewards start to control us, rather than our controlling the material things, that problems begin to arise.

Physical Indicators for the Trait of Possessiveness

Referring first to the basic motivational characteristics of somatotyping, the mesoendo will, generally speaking, be the least possessive of the five body types. Being freedom lovers, whose theme song is "Don't fence me in," the mesoendos appreciate their need to do their thing and usually allow others to have that same freedom.

The mesoecto is by far the most possessive of the five categories, as a group. Their need for security often manifests itself in possessiveness. They also have the most difficult time changing when it is necessary.

The mesomorphs are the second most possessive of the five categories. Although there are many different motivations to the mesomorph character, they generally are quite possessive. They relate to material things, and often this carries over to their personal relationships. The saving grace for the mesomorph is their great practical nature, which allows for change in their character once they realize they are overly possessive.

Contrary to popular belief, the ectomorph is not necessarily possessive in nature. Although their basic motivation is security, and most would assume this would lead to possessiveness, their passion for knowledge outweighs their need for possessions. This group is the "loner" group, and only when their security is threatened do they seem more possessive.

The endomorph is not overly possessive, as a group, and they rank alongside the ectomorph (as a group) in their amount of possessiveness. When endomorphs are possessive, it will be usually of their homes and what is in them. Remember, to the endomorphs their home is their castle. They will be possessive of the "creature comforts" or the things that make life easier for them. Their generosity and love of life keep them from being possessive of people.

Although somatotyping gives us the general categories of possessiveness, the study of face language and jewelry gives us the specific area and degree of possessiveness in the individual. First, let's look at jewelry. The greater amount of adornment with the use of jewelry, the more possessive of material things the person will be. Quite often this will carry over to the desire to possess people as well. This is one of the best indicators of just how possessive an individual is. As an augmenting trait, it is a must to observe.

Now let's turn to *primary* keys to possessiveness. A primary indicator is the way in which the ear attaches to the head. We realize that most of you are saying, "You've got to be kidding. What does the way the ear attaches to my head have to do with being possessive?" Well, it has been verified by many many studies and case histories—it is a validated trait. Okay, then what do you look for?

When viewing the ear from the front, you look to see how it appears to come out the head. If the ear appears to sit in a cup or indentation on the side of the head, you are seeing a person who is not at all possessive. If the ear appears to be attached even with the side of the head, then you are seeing what is considered as average. If, on the other hand, the ear appears to sit on a ledge, then you are viewing a person who is quite possessive. We rate this trait on a scale of one to ten. One is not possessive at all, and ten is the extremely possessive person. Of the illustrations, "A" equals one, "B" equals a five or average, and "C" is equal to ten, which is the extremely possessive person. Refer to page 56.

It is important to weigh all the factors before deciding just where and how much this trait indicates. To view only the ear and then say a person is possessive, just might be totally wrong. It is important to know the other augmenting traits to possessiveness.

Vanity is a possible augmenting trait, since jealousy is often a form of vanity, and vanity is often a form of possessiveness. Vain people rarely like others taking what they consider to be theirs.

Another augmenting trait to possessiveness is the straight or Roman nose and the hook or Scrooge nose. Since these both indicate an ability to handle money, they would relate to possessiveness in material things, which could lead to possessiveness in people. Conversely, the turned-up nose on the nonpossessive individual is an augmenting trait in the other direction—indicating a lack of possessiveness.

The very small iris (colored part of the eye) usually is found on the extremely unemotional person. This corresponds to the possessive individual in the following manner. The small iris is found on those who operate on the principal of "dog eat dog, and I'll get mine first." This leads to a possessive nature in a person. Small-iris people are generally more self-centered individuals.

Two other augmenting traits to possessiveness are the thin-lipped person and the acutely stubborn person. Although these last two are relatively minor indicators, they still are of importance. For very obvious reasons, the more augmenting traits apparent, the greater the degree of possessiveness.

The indicators for lack of possessiveness are usually totally opposite of those for possessiveness. If an individual has the following: mesoendo body type, thick lips, large iris, sunken ears, and no apparent degree of vanity, then you have a giver who probably doesn't have anything to give, in that this person has already given away whatever he or she had. If poorly dressed, with no display of jewelry, then he or she may not have ever had anything to begin with! Remember—excesses on either side of the coin usually lead to trouble and misunderstandings.

Possessiveness may come in many forms, such as jealousy, greed, frugality, tyranny, power, or it may manifest itself in the form of fear of rejection. Possessiveness traits can create serious problems in our daily lives, especially in dealing with friends, lovers, or mates. In a situation in which one person is possessive and one is not, the stage is often set for tragedy.

Picture, if you will, the following situation. A very pos-sessive male meets a nonpossessive female. At first, all is well. She enjoys all the attention being showered on her. He in turn thinks she is madly in love with him because of her response to his attentions. Soon, as the relationship develops, she feels hemmed in and finds that whatever she does must be accom-panied by an explanation. The same attention she so readily admired at first is now crushing her. He, on the other hand, cannot understand why she doesn't appreciate all that he has done for her, especially since it was done in the name of love. Then in total frustration, she "observes" another male, and he comes unglued! Jealousy has now set in, and the relationship is headed for problems.

To reiterate a point made earlier, the choice of our friends, lovers, or mates is the least analytical, least logical of all our decisions. We are far more demanding and critical of the information we need to purchase an automobile than we are in choosing relationships. Yet, automobiles last us only a few years, and we expect our relationships to last a lifetime. Somehow or another, I feel we have our priorities mixed up.

In the choice of relationships, emotion is the guiding factor. Emotion and gut-level feelings should not be ignored, merely tempered with a bit of logic and reason. Any decision based on emotion, tempered with logic and reason, and supported by sufficient knowledge is a more efficient and practical tool in the decision-making process, guaranteeing better results. The more information and facts we gather and analyze about our friends, lovers, and mates, the more intelligently we can deal with them. The more we understand, the better we can relate and communicate. The better we communicate, the more pleasant and long lasting will be the relationship.

The importance of being able to recognize the personality trait of possessiveness cannot be overemphasized. It is of profound significance in our personal relationships.

Possessiveness may be either excessive or totally lacking in a person's personality. In either case, a variety of problems can exist as a result. A lack of possessiveness, combined with generosity in a personality, could result in a person being somewhat negligent in financial affairs and could prove disasterous in a family situation. This can destroy a relationship as quickly as the overly possessive situation can. A little imagination can easily show what might happen if a man who was overly generous and nonpossessive married a very possessive woman. Many arguments would be created over his being generous to others, making his family do without. Jealousy would also be created by his giving his time away to others, not spending enough of it at home. This could easily create a great deal of insecurity for the wife. She may feel "He doesn't care about me." At best this would be a difficult marital situation. If the situation involved possessiveness of people only and not material things, jealousy of time and attention would certainly be a factor. There is no swifter destroyer of human happiness than sexual jealousy. The alarmingly high rate of divorce in today's society is an indication of the lack of understanding between mates. Knowledge and use of Body Talk could go a long way toward curbing this divorce rate.

Possessiveness is often carried over into the relationship of parents and their children. This can manifest itself in many ways. Most common is the overly possessive parent who becomes, in turn, overprotective. When children from such backgrounds grow up, they often have difficulty in facing the realities of the world. Another example of parental possessiveness is seen when one parent overpossesses a child and uses that as an excuse to drive a wedge between his or her spouse. Often this is due to an inability to possess the mate, therefore, this parent uses the child as a means of filling his or her needs.

Women's liberation is another good example of rebellion against possessiveness. It is very nice and important to be wanted, but no one wants to be possessed or owned as though she were an inanimate object, and yet this so often is the case. This destroys individual self-respect and self-esteem that is so vital to everyone's psychological needs. The E.R.A. movement is another example of rejection of the feeling of being owned that has its roots deeply implanted in possessiveness.

Another social problem wherein the seeds of overpossessiveness may be found as an important factor is the rising rate of family crimes. Child abuse and wife beating are two crimes of personal assault very common in our society where possessiveness is often the major cause. A jealous man may beat his wife, trying to prevent her from showing affection to their children. This feeling of "You love the child more than me" is not an uncommon reason given for either child or wife abuse. Along with the physical abuse so often used, comes mental abuse because of possessiveness. This is far more widespread than the physical abuse. Constant nagging is a good example of the mental abuse caused by possessiveness, for do we not get jealous when someone looks at or attempts to take from us what we consider to be ours?

Possessiveness as a personality trait is relevant to each of us in varying degrees in our daily lives and personal relationships. It is the extremes of this trait that elicit the severe social problems mentioned.

This discussion is intended to emphasize the importance of possessiveness and its understanding, so that when it is found to exist in someone we deal with, or in our own selves, we can more intelligently cope with it. This trait can be diminished and controlled when it is dealt with intelligently, but first it must be recognized as a factor in personal relationships. Left unchecked, possessiveness is a tremendous factor in creating anti-social behavior.

Once again, the importance of knowledge and understanding of our friend's, lover's, or mate's personality comes with a better understanding of their nonverbal indicators, and the understanding of possessiveness is one of the two most important traits. Many times it has been said, "love is blind," and this is so true. If we can start using some analytical powers to augment our emotional reasoning, then our society has a chance to prosper in the fields of human and social behavior.

12
Recognizing Pressure Signs

Smooth seas never make a skillful mariner, nor does uninterrupted prosperity and success ensure one's usefulness and happiness. Adversity and problems are the state wherein we may best come to know ourselves. It is the first step on the pathway to truth. All too often we fail to see the reason and the necessity of problems in our daily lives. Only unsolved problems are stumbling blocks on the path to progress. Problems for which we find solutions are a blessing when we perceive the lessons and benefits we receive from them. Every problem brings with it the key to its solution, and every adversity is the diamond dust used by God to cut and polish His rough diamonds.

Often in our complex and frustrating society, with its ever-increasing rapid pace, tension, and problems, we witness people burdened with problems for which no solution has yet been found. Body Talk can help us recognize people under pressure, and from this knowledge we can gain an understanding of how to relate to them and give suggestions for dealing with it. There are those who live under great pressure but have the ability to cope with it, and there are those who do not have this ability. The primary facial indicator for pressure problems is what the Japanese call *san paku*. In Japanese this means "three whites." It indicates the areas of the eye in which you normally see white to the left and the right of the iris with white visible also underneath the iris.

San paku is caused by pressure created within the mind resulting in a change in the muscles that roll the eye upward in the socket, exposing the white of the eye under the iris of the eye. White showing under the iris of *one eye*, when you look straight into the face in a level position, indicates an accident-prone condition, which may be considered as an accident looking for a place to happen. This condition can and often does illustrate a basic left-right trait, indicating pressure in one side of your life, either personal and private or public and business, for which a solution has not yet been found.

Remember that the right upper portion of the face controls the left lower portion. So, if you have a headache that is manifested on the right side, it will affect the left eye, or vice versa. When the tension created in the mind affects the optic nerves and muscles, rolling back the eye in the socket, the effect will be a loss of peripheral vision and depth perception. This will not be great enough to affect the accuracy of vision, but the loss of peripheral vision and depth perception will be enough to create the possibility of bumping into things and misjudging the position of objects. This can be very dangerous while driving. This is what makes one accident-prone. Whenever this condition is seen, caution is advisable. Check yourself in the mirror in the morning, in a relaxed state while dressing. If you see the white of the eye showing under one eye or if one eye is higher up in the socket than the other, know that your vision may be off and be careful. If you know you are under pressure and there is little difference showing, be aware that your vision may be affected.

San paku may show up in both eyes. This condition indicates pressure in both sides of your life or pressure on one side so great that both sides of the brain are affected so that both eyes react, showing white under both irises. When you see someone with this condition, it is important to realize you are dealing with someone living under great pressure. Therefore, it is best to try to relate to that person with this problem in mind. Be understanding, sympathetic, and try to be helpful. Do not discuss your problems, for this would only add to the pressure and depress him or her more. This also indicates a need to be careful, and caution should be advised as to the possibility of accidents.

The next trait to look for when *san paku* is present in both eyes is whether the eye is glassy, glazed over, or staring blankly. If this is the case, be very careful. This is the fugacity or melancholy look. What this person is saying nonverbally is "My problems and pressures are so great I cannot visualize what is happening. My mind is not with us." If half the iris is obscured by white showing under the iris, this indicates the person is hiding something as well. Usually when this is evident, the person has his or her mind on whatever is being suppressed or hidden. This person is not dealing with reality. Whenever you see someone with the three whites showing in both eyes, having a glazed, blank look, with half the iris obscured, you will know this person is under tremendous pressure. There is something being suppressed in the dark recesses of the mind; this person is mentally not there. This type person can become schizophrenic, or psychotic.

There are those who can handle pressure and those who cannot. Those who seem to thrive on pressure frequently are found in certain professions or occupations that inherently have a fast pace and pressure. Invariably, if the person has arched eyebrows and fits in the category of meso or mesoendo, this type seems to thrive on pressure. This type also develops ulcers often. These people seem to desire or even need a fast pace and pressure in their lives. They can handle it and seem to work well under it. If you are one of this type and live under a lot of pressure, it might be well to re-evaluate your life-style and slow down a bit, even though you can function well under pressure. A news commentator I know on television has *san paku* under both eyes. He is obviously under a lot of pressure but evidently functions well under it. Even so, you can tell when he has a good day or bad day by the amount of whites showing under the iris. This changes daily with him.

If mesos, mesoectos, endomorphs, or ectomorphs having the flat eyebrow that indicates the need for harmony show white under the iris, they are placed in a precarious situation. Their need for harmony is so ingrained into their nature that when placed in a disharmonious situation, they tend to become unglued. This is especially true for the mesomorphs, since this type also hates to lose. If half the iris is obscured or the eye is glazed, at this point be careful in your dealings. If you cannot help them, at least be careful not to antagonize them.

Recognizing the indicators for pressure problems should be of great value for teachers, for often *san paku* will be seen in disturbed children or children with emotional problems either at home or school. Perhaps the child with *san paku* is not understanding what is being taught, and because of apprehension, desire for good grades, and parental favor he may feel pressured. This could be a signal for the teacher to give more personal attention to the child and to relate to his or her problems better. An unhappy home life or peer group relations may be the problem, but whatever the cause, just realizing there is pressure will help find a solution and create better relations between teacher and student. Often young people who use drugs will demonstrate *san paku*. It is often manifested by fear of detection, rather than pressure. Often young people who turn to drugs do so out of a desire to escape from pressure in their lives, from a restless inability to cope with reality.

Eyes such as those of Charles Manson are a good example of what the Chinese call wolf eye. This is where whites of the eye show above the iris as well as on both sides. When this is accompanied with a glazed, brittle, hard stare, it is known as the diabolical eye. The diabolical eye is not often seen, and it is one you hope never to encounter.

Each of the Charles Manson followers showed *san paku* under the iris, and the glazed, brittle stare was evident. They had that vacant expression in their eyes, and all of them were known to be heavy users of drugs. Although they realized that what they were doing was wrong, they felt no remorse or compassion for their victims. The Manson group lived in a totally unreal world of their own, characterized by a dependence on drugs, following the dictates of Manson, and their only law was to please him. It showed in their eyes.

It is interesting to note that those who commit crimes without compunction do not show *san paku*, because within their belief system they have done nothing wrong. Therefore, they do not build up the pressure problems and feel no guilt. This is the true criminal mind at work, showing no remorse, guilt, or compassion. These criminals often have glazed or glassy eyes with eyelids drooping over the eye, indicating that they are hiding their actions.

San paku is one of the most important of the nonverbal indicators. It is one of the traits most often seen in our complex and fast-paced society. All of us at one time or another experience pressure in our lives. Some of us are better able to handle it than others. Being able to recognize pressure problems in ourselves and in others is a very important factor in our personal relationships. Some people will not admit they live under pressure. This has been pointed out in counseling people who had every indication of pressure problems. Even though they knew that problems and pressures were tremendous, they would not admit it. Failure to do so, however, aggravated an existing condition and prevented finding a solution. Being aware is the first step in solving the problem. It is no disgrace to have problems. The disappointment comes in having them and not being able to cope with them in an intelligent manner. Self-awareness, self-improvement, and improvement of relationships with others are the fruits found in the orchard of nonverbal communications.

13
Love, Romance and Body Talk

Romance is the canvas supplied by Nature that is embroidered by the imagination of those who love to be in love. Love and romance are often thought to be synonymous, because they are closely associated. However, this is not always true. Romance is the picturesque, fanciful imagery drawn from the imagination of the romantic mind so well suited to the atmosphere of budding love that it becomes at once the spice and the prelude to romantic love. The drama of love is played on the stage of romance. It is the imagery, the setting, the lighting, and the choreography set to music, creating the atmosphere that enhances the enactment of the most rewarding of the human emotions—love.

The incurable romantic is the prized jewel in the treasure of mankind. These people give variety, enthusiasm, and vitality to life. Blessed be the romantics—for they are the spice of life.

Romance has been so much a part of the American scene that each of us has been programmed to appreciate the importance of it in our lives. Few actually understand the anatomy of romance and the profound need for it or the effect it has on our lives. Understanding it in relationships is very important. The incurable romantic sees life from a broader perspective than others. Nothing is simple or mundane. They embellish everything with the fruits of vivid imagination.

The large, emotional eye is the first characteristic trait of the incurable romantic. Second is the highly arched eyebrow, indicating a dramatic life-style. Third is the up-turned nose, indicating the helpers who want to give of themselves. Fourth is the tip of the nose being turned up, indicating an open-minded nature. Fifth are the very thick lips of the generous, automatic giver. Sixth are the high cheekbones, the sign of adventure.

These basic indicators are the prime characteristics of the incurable romantic. As in judging all other indicators, rate these traits on a one-to-ten basis to determine the degree of romantic nature. Should you find someone with a rating of ten on each trait, you will indeed be fortunate, for you will have found an incurable romantic personified. If you are involved in a relationship with a person such as this, you are very lucky. Life will never be dull. These people bring joy and happiness into your life. Don't let one like this get away from you if you are fortunate enough to know one—for they are rare.

Relating to incurable romantics is a lesson well worth learning. The key is understanding that incurable romantics create in their mind the romantic atmosphere they desire and seek out in all aspects of their lives. They desire constant adventure, variety, action, and new and varied exciting places, always set in the romantic atmosphere of soft lights and music. Exotic places appeal to the romantic nature. The romantics love to be in love; therefore, they like and need to feel they are wanted, desirable, attractive, and loved in return. They exist for days of wine and roses. Help the incurable romantics to fulfill these expectations. Give them lots of attention. Surprise them with unexpected gifts, flowers, perfume, candle-lit dinners, good wine, exotic foods, new and unusual places. Always guard against routine. If you appreciate the same things in life and show it, they will gladly share their lives, bringing joy into what might otherwise have been a commonplace existence.

In sexual relationships, the incurable romantics will assume these same attitudes and will display the same desires that are expressed in all their other actions. Experimentation, variety, and surprises are necessary aspects of the romantic nature. Don't fall into a rut. Perfunctory sex does not appeal to the romantic, and boredom is a fatal disease.

Sex to the incurable romantic should be as punctuation is to poetry. It should emphasize, elucidate, and set the meter, which culminates a beautiful verse. The mood and setting, the atmosphere and passion should be properly stimulated and expressed in new, varied, and exciting ways, always in harmony with the romantic nature.

Generally speaking, it is best to look for traits similar to yours when choosing a mate or friendship partner, because the more differences in personality, the more understanding and adjustment will be required for a harmonious relationship. If you are not an incurable romantic and want to become more romantic in nature, an awareness of the characteristics related here will aid in developing a romantic nature, with sufficient concentration of will and a conscientious effort. If you are not this type by nature and you are in a relationship with someone who is, relate to these basic traits and try to harmonize with them to create a mutually rewarding relationship.

The Nonverbal Keys to Sex

Throughout our relationships with others we often try to figure out why we seem to fail at understanding our friends', lovers', or mates' sexual needs. Many of the problems can be solved by understanding the nonverbal keys to sex.

Fear of rejection keeps people from expressing their needs and desires in sexual matters. They allow their relationship to deteriorate, because they are afraid to share the basic ways they wish to be treated sexually. Obviously, this has to be a two-way street, with each partner deferring to the other at some time or another, but a basic understanding will allow you to relate without having to express your desires in words.

A cautionary note is in order. Be sure you look for the augmenting traits that reinforce each other. If you see a primary trait and nothing to back it up, then be very cautious, as this may not apply to that person from a sexual standpoint.

The traits relating to sexuality are the same ones for other parts of the personality. All we are going to do is apply them to a situation evolving around sexual relations.

Small Iris Versus Large Iris

The size of the iris indicates the degree of outward emotion that is displayed. The smaller the iris, the quicker you get to the point. Don't waste time with a lot of foreplay, for it will not be appreciated. People with a very large iris demand a great deal of foreplay. They relate to emotion and like to take their time savoring each moment of this type of ecstacy.

Wide-set Eyes

The wide-set eyes indicate broad-minded people, and they view their sex the same way, very broad mindedly! They take things at an easygoing pace, and therefore you normally don't want to rush them.

Eyes Set Close Together

Close-set eyes indicate those who go by the book. With these individuals you must be careful not to skip over anything that is expected. They tend to be perfectionists, and they can be hard to please. We suggest you let a person like this lead, and just follow that lead.

Flat Eyebrows

"In harmony all the way" should be the credo of the flat-eyebrowed person. They like teamwork and harmony and will respond accordingly.

Arched (Dramatic) Eyebrows

People with arched (dramatic) eyebrows enjoy things differently, and variety is considered the spice of life in their style of lovemaking. The dramatic people can fantasize better than any other category, and they love to fulfill their fantasies. If you are in a relationship with this type of person, don't restrict your lovemaking to the bedroom. Rather, vary both the location and the way you make love.

High Eyebrows

When courting a person with eyebrows that sit very high over the eyes, be aware that this person needs to have privacy in an expression of affection. People with this trait probably won't want you even to kiss them in public, let alone express any other form of love openly. Put this individual in private surroundings and it is a horse of another color!

Small Mouth

Remember the small mouth? This is the introverted type of individual who will tend to be brief and efficient in lovemaking, because of not wanting to share the personality hidden inside. This is mostly a secondary trait in understanding sexual response, and rarely is it considered a primary trait.

Loose Mouth or Large Mouth

People with the loose or large mouth are extroverts, and they tend to be impetuous. They have a lot of fun and will act spontaneously during lovemaking. Also, they will most often act on the spur of the moment, preferring that to a long planned-out evening.

Thick Lips

Thick lips indicate generosity, and in sexual relationships this transcribes into a lot of foreplay. The people who are generous in nature enjoy their sex and like to savor it as long as possible.

135

Broad Face Versus Narrow Face

As mentioned earlier, the broader the face, the greater the degree of self-confidence, and the narrower the face, the lesser the degree of self-confidence. The same holds true in applying this trait toward sexual aggressiveness. The broader the face, the more self-confident a person will be sexually. These people will be sure of themselves and know what they are doing. The narrower the face, the greater the need for coaxing. Don't come on too strong too quickly with the narrow-faced person or you will shut him or her out in a hurry.

Soft Body

The soft body is slower to respond and therefore needs more foreplay. With this person take your time and get the full enjoyment that is offered.

Hard Body

These people seem to be very quick to respond. They are more efficient, faster on the trigger, and need less foreplay.

Thin-skinned, Delicate Types

Always love those with thin skin before making love to them! Treat them with gentleness, and again, never rush into things. Let this type of person set the pace.

Now then, why not put some of these combinations together and see how they augment themselves. You might even take a mirror and see how they apply to you. Above all, be honest with yourself.

Many of the other traits also apply to the art of making love. It only takes your own expertise at recognizing grabber traits and learning to relate to them to improve your own abilities. If ever the statement "To give is better than to receive" applied to an art, it is to this one.

Little Things That Mean a Lot

Quite often in man-woman relationships the little differences have a tendency to add up until they are major problems. These "little" differences are the basic differences in personality that were not considered when the relationship first started. We all view things from our own perspective, and rarely do we see things as others do—especially when it involves ourselves. This is not to say that these differences are by any means wrong. Quite the contrary, they are very necessary. It is our understanding of them that needs to be brought to the forefront.

With a basic understanding of Body Talk you will at least be aware of where some of the differences are, and how they are likely to affect any relationship. We will list a few of these basic differences and how they could affect a relationship.

Let us take a male with an objective forehead and a lot of eyelid showing, and couple that with a woman who has a subjective forehead and the very analytical eyelid (no eyelid visible at all). On the male's side of the coin you have a person who makes decisions quickly and will tend to overcome any obstacles he encounters as he goes along. He is a real action person; a doer who doesn't worry about how to do things. Rather, he relies on his ability to cope with a situation as it develops. The female, on the other hand, never makes a decision without first using thought processes. She is a thinker and relies heavily on using her brain power to keep her out of difficult situations. Being subjective in nature, as well as being analytical, causes her to delay making any decision until she has thoroughly weighed all the parameters that surround her decision. She will take any time necessary to make this decision and will resent being hurried into a fast response.

Now put these two together getting ready to go out for the evening. The male has the car started and is ready to leave, but the female is still considering what she wants to wear! First thing you know an argument has started. He is saying hurry up, and she is complaining about being rushed. This then becomes one little wedge of unhappiness between them. The later it becomes the more agitated he becomes at the delays, while she is irritated at his persistence. Finally, when they do leave the house he starts driving in a hurry, which further aggravates her already worried state, and she asks him to slow down. The ensuing discussion develops into "You don't love me or you would be more sensitive to my wants and needs" type of comments, each blaming the other, and all because they both failed to take into consideration basic differences in each of their personalities.

A simpler approach would be to have her prepare herself earlier, or have him sit down and watch a television show while waiting. Better still, she might involve him in her decisions as to what to wear, how to fix her hair, and the like. By utilizing each other's differences in personality traits this negative scene could be turned into a positive one that would increase the love and respect rather than drive that wedge between them. His utilization of her ability to think things out and work with logic and reason might keep him out of trouble or at least save some of his energies, whereas his ability to make quick decisions would assist her and cut down on needless worry.

This is just one small application of this basic difference. There are many more that could be discussed. Think of how many times in your own life you were victim of this "I act but you think, or you act while I think" syndrome, and how it affected you. Think also of some of the augmenting traits to add further to this type of misunderstanding. Such traits as the trait for caution, stubbornness, emotion, sensitivity, and pressure could increase or decrease the degree of this problem.

Armed with this type of knowledge you can now apply this to the everyday situations you run into. For example, if you are a salesperson and you see a customer who has the subjective forehead and the analytical eyelid, give that person time to consider what you are saying in your selling presentation. Don't press for a quick decision, because you will probably lose the sale if you do. Conversely, if the forehead is extremely objective and you see a lot of eyelid, you can be assured this person can make up his or her mind while you are talking. The doer type of person rarely wants to think about it overnight, preferring to make a decision at the time, so that he or she may go on to other things.

If you were an employer, you wouldn't hire the objective doer type to do complicated research that demanded concentration and patience in thought process, nor would you hire the subjective thinker to get a rush job done in a hurry.

The manager who at five minutes to five requires a letter typed and into the mail by five shouldn't expect the subjective thinker to get it done without problems or mistakes, because it will worry that same person and cause great anxiety. Instead, ask the objective doer in the group to please get it out.

If you are the subjective-thinker type of sales manager, don't expect the objective-doer salespersons to be good at paperwork. They will get the job done for you, but don't overburden this type with tedious paperwork that they feel takes away from selling time.

To sum it all up, this knowledge will give you as Robert Burns so wisely stated, "The gift to see ourselves as others see us."

Automatic Responsiveness

How sensitive we are to our surroundings plays an important part in our everyday lives and often will contribute greatly to misunderstandings between people. Special awareness of those traits that deal with responsiveness will lead to a greater understanding of ourselves as well as understanding of others. When these traits augment themselves, then awareness levels of responsiveness are definitely increased.

Let us first look at those traits that would make us more responsive or sensitive to our surroundings and what takes place within those surroundings. The first trait to consider would be the skin sensitivity. People with thin skin are sensitive to physical and verbal abuse to a high degree. The best way to tell how sensitive you are in relation to others is to determine how you react to suntanning. If you are one of those people who steps into the sun and burns quickly, then you are of the extreme sensitivity. If, while getting a tan, you usually stay out too long the first time and burn, but do not burn on succeeding attempts to tan, you would be considered to be about average in sensitivity. If you can go out in the sun and just tan, never seeming to burn, you have a high resistance to sensitivity. Remember also, the more sensitive you are to physical pain, the more sensitive you will be to verbal abuse.

Add to this the large iris or emotional type of person. Next add the people whose eyes are wide open, who see everything around them and respond more quickly to a given stimulus. Still further, add narrow-set eyes that turn up toward the outer portion. People with these traits are not critical but believe in following the rules. Add still another augmenting trait, that of the dramatic eyebrow, which indicates someone who sees things fully and with embellishments.

The traits for sympathy would also increase responsiveness, as would the person with very fine hair. Add a person with loose skin texture who lacks self-confidence, and you have a super-sensitive personality that will react or respond to almost anything. Caution with what you say or do around this person would be the order of the day, so to speak. He or she will most likely overreact.

The reverse would combine the following traits. Thick, taut skin, coarse hair, small irises, thin lips, partially closed eyes (squinted look), wide-set eyes, flat eyebrows, down-turned eyes (criticalness), and a broad face, indicating self-confidence. This person is not going to be as responsive or sensitive to either verbal or physical abuse. Can you imagine what marriage would be like with two people of these opposite traits? Yet we see it every day, and we wonder why the divorce rate is so high.

Being aware of the other person's characteristics could assist all of us in our daily lives, both personal and business.

Are These Traits Changeable or Am I Stuck With Them

All of the traits mentioned are very definitely changeable. I am often asked, in the seminars we do around the country, if the facial features will change as the personality changes. Again, the answer is yes. However, it takes time. There are some traits that can become so ingrained in the facial structure that it would take years to change them. Usually there will be some changes in the augmenting traits as well, and often they will indicate a personality change before the basic trait does.

Take the person who has thick, taut skin, for example, who wants to become more sensitive to his or her surroundings. The thickness of the skin may not change very rapidly, taking maybe a year or two to thin—if indeed it does become thin. However, the change of attitude, becoming more sensitive to his or her surroundings, will change the tautness of the skin rather rapidly. Other indicators will also change, and probably the most noticeable of all the traits to change will be the eyes. As we attempt to change our personalities, and in so doing change our features, the eye plays the most important role. Whether it be in a softening of attitudes or a hardening of attitudes, the eye will be the first place to register the change. This is why we, as a society, depend on how a person "looks" at us. So much information can be transmitted by the eye.

Which comes first, the chicken or the egg? Again, this is one of the most frequently asked questions at seminars. Do the physical traits change first, or does the personality have to change first? And what about cosmetic surgery? Does the personality change if cosmetic surgery has been done?

A positive statement to these questions would be ridiculous. First of all it depends on the situation. Generally, the personality will change first, then the physical indicator will change. I have seen cases in which excessive weight loss changed the personality, but the personality did not change until after the weight was lost. In the case of facial traits, the answer is yes. The personality usually changes first, but even here one must be careful, for a heart attack can change both physical features as well as personality, overnight! It doesn't happen often, but it does happen.

It is also possible for the cosmetic changes to backfire. Remember, others may not know the specifics of nonverbal communication, yet they react to it subconsciously. We may not know the reason why we react as we do, but we do react.

This was brought home to me in some marriage counseling I have done. It involved a case in which a woman had had a nose bob done, changing her nose from a hook (or money nose) to the up-turned (helper) nose. No other features were changed, and in this case she was not trying to change her personality. She was very successful in business before she had the nose operation and could not understand why people were constantly trying to take advantage of her when they hadn't done so before. She found people asking her to do things she never would have been asked prior to her operation. It was still evident in looking at her overall personality and her augmenting features that she had not changed and become more giving of herself, as there were no augmenting traits to support the helper nose. However, most people reacted to what was the most apparent feature rather than understanding the total image.

When I explained to the woman the reasons people acted the way they did, she almost wished she hadn't had the operation. She is still very successful; however, she has to work harder to overcome other people's attitudes toward her, especially where it concerns money. The rewarding side to this is that in her personal life others have a different view of her, and she finds this comforting, even though she is adamant about not changing her personality.

Another often-asked question is about those features that are sometimes painted on with the aid of cosmetics. Such things as eyebrows and lip lines can be altered with the use of cosmetics. It has been our observation that what is painted on is what is desired in the personality. For example, the eyebrow that is plucked on the bottom, then painted or extended on the top describes someone who wants to be treated with more formality. Also, we often see more of an arch (dramatic) added to the eyebrow than was there originally. Although we cannot say this is always the case, it does appear that in at least 85 percent of those cases studied, the change made was what was desired in the personality.

The final area of noticeable change occurs when there has been a tremendous philosophical change. This can be brought on by almost anything. We have studied a number of cases in which a heart attack or knowledge of a serious disease has changed the philosophical viewpoint. Most frequently the change has evolved around the personality traits of possessiveness and money handling, as it affects generosity. Over and over again we have seen people once concerned with money suffering a heart attack, for example, then realizing they can't take their money with them, becoming magnanimous overnight. The physical traits do not often change with this philosophical change, at least not very quickly.

Sometimes no immediate apparent physical changes take place, and at other times they do. The area in which you will notice the change is, again, the eye. There is a softness that develops in the gaze that indicates a change has taken place.

At the loss of a loved one we have noticed a rapid change in aloofness. This shows up in the heightening of the eyebrow and can occur quickly, but usually it will return to its normal status over a period of time as the person adjusts to the changes in life-style.

I have not found one trait that is not changeable from a physical point of view. Some changes take a great deal of time; however, our research has indicated that all the traits will eventually change if the personality has changed.

How to Use Body Talk in Choosing Your Mate

As we indicated at the start of this book, most relationships are founded on gut-level feelings. I would be the last person in this world to indicate that this method is wrong. That instant charisma that exists between two people should never be overlooked. We would add to this feeling or charisma the knowledge of Body Talk. The advantage you would gain is immeasurable, in that you would start the relationship with a very basic knowledge of the primary traits of the personality of your partner. It would assist everyone using it in understanding the potential areas of conflict prior to those same conflicts developing.

If you are a possessive person, prone toward jealousy, then in seeking another individual you might look for the same

143

characteristics. Thus you could have an understanding going into the relationship that the two of you would possess each other, thereby eliminating some of the jealousy that might cause problems. If you are unemotional, then look for someone who is also unemotional, who will relate in a similar fashion to a given set of stimuli. This is the area in which Body Talk can be of most assistance.

We certainly do not advocate that it would be wise to choose a friend, lover, or mate solely by Body Talk, for the hidden feelings still must come into play in this type of a decision. However, key traits might be desirable to know in order to choose wisely.

The best way is to first look in a mirror and determine your own strong points. Be honest with yourself in evaluating these traits. Look for the strengths and also those areas that you are not happy with. Remember, this science is not an absolute; it can be wrong in certain cases, so do not overjudge yourself. Then when you have determined your own strengths, plan in your own mind what strengths you most desire in another. You may wish to evaluate those traits that *you* consider to be weaknesses in yourself and list those as the opposite of what you seek in another individual. In other words, if you rate yourself as a one on a given trait and you would like to be a ten, then you might look for someone who is a ten on that trait.

After you have determined what traits to seek in another, list them by importance. What strengths do you admire the most? Those should be listed first.

We have found through our research that the greater the similarity in face language, the stronger the relationship. The exceptions to this come when those similarities are considered weaknesses by both persons, and they blame each other for those weaknesses. On certain traits it is good to match strengths with weaknesses, and on other traits this just compounds the problems.

Look also for the traits *you* dislike the most and watch out for those traits, especially if they are very high in the other person. If you already have your lover, friend, or mate, then use this knowledge to give you a better understanding of that person. I do not suggest that you try to confront the other person with the knowledge that a trait is wrong, because in his or her eyes it may be considered a strength. Rather, share your findings in a neutral way, not suggesting right or wrong, and bring this information into the open. After all, isn't that what we are all trying to do—learning to communicate with those we care about? At least the channels of communication will have been opened, and unless the trait you are discussing is one for stubbornness, you should both gain insight from this type of communication.

Integrity

I have often been asked to come up with a trait or traits for integrity. To my knowledge, there are no specific traits to determine honesty; however, there are traits, or combinations of traits, that do indicate dishonesty.

The reason there are no given traits for honesty is because everyone has a different opinion of honesty. The mother who steals food for her children to keep them from starving may not be considered dishonest in some circles. The business person who has been able to undersell the competition and put them out of business is considered shrewd, not dishonest, even though that person may have used tactics that may not be considered ethical. The bank robber who works with accomplices, although stealing from the general public, wouldn't dream of cheating the accomplices out of their share and therefore would be considered by those same accomplices as an honest person. Is the politician who falls under the influence of a powerful lobbyist and because of that pressure decides in favor of that lobbyist's favorite legislation being honest or dishonest? You can see that honesty is in the eye of the beholder, to a great extent.

The traits for dishonesty are apparent, because they represent the person's own belief system and show up in individuals when they are being dishonest with another. These traits are augmentative and will often reinforce themselves as the extent of dishonesty is increased. A word of caution. Be sure

145

that in watching for these traits what you see is in fact a trait for dishonesty, not one born from fear. Often the two have been confused.

The first trait to look for in noting dishonesty is what we call the shifty eye, the person who will not look you square in the eye and hold the contact. Remember, the inability to look you in the eye is not based on subconscious fear. The fear could be caused by things other than those associated with dishonesty. Usually, however, the shifty-eyed person will also have an augmentative trait apparent—squinty eye that goes along with the shifty eye. When a person will not hold your gaze and the eyes start to close as in a squint, then you are seeing someone who desires to deceive you. If, in addition to the first two traits there is a slight smile at the corners of the mouth, then it is a further indication of deception.

You might like to try an experiment to ascertain just what this combination looks like. Take a mirror and look into it in a normal relaxed manner. Now concentrate your mental powers on the most devious, deceitful thing you have ever done, allowing your facial muscles to form naturally, and take another look into the mirror. Notice that the eyelids came down over the eye, and the hint of a smile appeared on the corners of the mouth. If this does not show up on your face, you are a pretty good con-artist.

Another additional trait to look for is what the hands are saying during a conversation you suspect to be deceitful. Usually, the palms will be pointing down, away from the person. The dishonest person may also be quite fidgety; however, this may also be nervous energy. When you view a combination of all the above traits, beware! This person is really trying to get you.

Remember that this is a subconscious reaction that happens in all of us, and only the most skilled of the con-artists can overcome the normal reactions, appearing to be honest. Usually their signs of honesty are suspect, because they are practiced, rather than natural.

14
Grabber Traits

Now that you have all this good knowledge, how do you use it? What good can it do you? How do you remember all the traits?

In all of us there are certain traits that will appear to jump out at you. It is these traits to which you should respond. Each of us has at least a half dozen or more physical indicators that on a one-to-ten scale would register either one or ten. These are the grabber traits. They represent the basic personality and usually indicate the important areas of a person's thinking. They seem to shout "Look at me! This is what makes me tick." Combining these traits gives you a quick understanding of the other person and allows you to relate to him or her in a more proficient manner.

As you develop a relationship, you can determine any additional traits that would be important to you in understanding how a person will act or react to a given set of circumstances. The grabber traits are the ones to relate to initially.

In our society today we all have a tendency to see others only as they relate to us, rather than trying to see ourselves relating to them. We force them to our own interests, rather than finding out what their interests are, or at least finding a mutual interest. How often have you been involved in conversations that were totally meaningless to you? Why do you suppose people make fun about talking about the weather? Obviously, the weather, boring as it may be, is mutual ground and can be used to start a conversation. Wouldn't it be more exciting to discuss something common to both parties? If you know yourself from a nonverbal standpoint, then you can always find a similar trait in another person. This is called relating to the other person's comfort zone. To do this we will invent a hypothetical person.

A man, thirty-five, makes $50,000 income a year, drives a Lincoln Mark IV, is single, wears $300 suits, reads the Wall Street Journal, lives in a $1,000/month apartment, and has a sailboat for weekends. This man's comfort zones will be the top or bottom of his desires. What are his comfort zones? Let's take them one at a time.

First, he is thirty-five, and will probably not relate to children under fifteen well, or to old folks on welfare. He would not relate to anyone in the country, nor to the scrubby boots and jeans crowd of the small towns. He probably is not interested in reading *Ladies Home Journal*, and if you were talking to him about automobiles, he wouldn't relate well to Chevrolets or Volkswagens. He certainly isn't going to be interested in your fantastic savings on a $50 suit you got for only $39.95! What, then, is he interested in? Well, how about the stock market? How to handle a sailboat? The high cost of running a good automobile? His excellent taste in clothes, or his choice of fine wine? Ah! "But those things don't interest me," you say. Here is where the art of Body Talk comes in.

When you look at him you notice his extremely flat eyebrows and his relatively thick, tanned skin. Immediately you know that here is someone who likes a challenge, who is the outdoor type. You know he is well dressed, so you can expect good taste. How many subjects would be of mutual interest that involve sports, the outdoors, and good taste? These subjects now become the door openers that allow you to communicate effectively from the very beginning. Soon you will notice the other person inquiring about your interests because you showed an interest in him.

Sometimes called the mutual admiration society, the "you-first" method is the best way to meet new people and make sincere new friends. Communication is the key to understanding, and understanding is the key to a beautiful relationship with another. When you place the other person's interests above yours, you have opened many doors. Now, let's apply the comfort zones to Body Talk.

The basic comfort zones in all of us are the grabber traits mentioned earlier. These are those traits that rate extremely high or low on our faces, the ones that shout silently at you. The best way to do this is to first know your own grabber traits. Then, when you look at a person you will know which traits you have in common. I would suggest you start at the eyes.

The eyes are the mirror of the mind and are definitely the most meaningful of all traits. Look first to see if there is any pressure present, and then look to see if the gaze is clear and unworried. After determining that, look at the size of the iris. Is it large, small, or average? Next look at the eyebrows; are they flat, rounded, or arched?

Next look at the lips. Are they thick or thin? Is the mouth large, small, or average? What shape is the nose—straight, up-turned, or hooked? Is the chin wedge-shaped, square, or in between? Is the skin tone hard or soft? Thick or thin? Does the person have high cheekbones?

What you have looked for will tell you, by degree, how much of the following rules that person's life: emotion, money, stubbornness, sensitivity, harmony, dramatic outlook, adventurousness, and generosity of self. Then look for any outstanding traits other than those mentioned. Usually there will be two or three other things that jump off the face at you. It may be the analytical eyelid, the possessive ear, the systematic brow ridge, or any other trait that stands out by itself.

The information you have now obtained can be put into practice in just a few seconds, and it will allow you to communicate more effectively. Practice this on your friends, whom you already know, as it will help you verify your information and also increase your ability to "read" other people. To assist you in determining the grabber traits, the end of this chapter deals with past presidents and their grabber traits. This will also help you to understand why politicians do what they do rather than what they say they will do.

Well-known Personalities

What you see may not be what you think you are getting! Some professionals are so very good at what they do, that you form opinions about them based on what you heard them say, rather than what they really are like out of their work atmosphere. I've chosen two well-known people that fit this mold very well indeed. Some of you will be very surprised at what their faces and bodies have to say, compared with the opinions you have formed.

Then after disecting the personalities of those two people, I have listed the major traits of a few of our more recent presidents and how they rate on a scale of one to ten (ten is high, one is low). Rather than detail each of them, I feel it would be fun for you to do your own analyzing, based on the earlier chapters in the book. Take each trait listed and cross reference it for yourself. I believe you will be both surprised and pleased at what you will find!

Good Bodytalking to you!!

Howard Cosell, televison-sportscaster, attorney, orator par excellence.

Here is one of my favorite personalities! The world is his stage, and does he have fun with it!

First the traits—

Harmony eyebrows 10, money or hook nose 10, analytical eyelids 10, large irises 8, eyebrows high over the eye 9, tact 10, skeptical nose tip 9, generosity 9, ability to handle authority and responsibility—business 10, personal 4, possessive ears 10, forward ego balance 10, and insatiable curiosity 10.

What you hear is not what his friends know! What goes on over television is an act, a staged play, a facade. Howard Cosell is a pussycat! He is not at all as he appears on television. He is warm, extremely sensitive, very emotional, a person who would rather hurt himself than see someone else get hurt. His verbal eloquence is a built-in protection against being hurt by others. My guess is that as a child he was somewhat introverted and developed the verbal skills to overcome a natural shyness. I doubt if many people know the real Howard, for he carefully guards his real personality. I sometimes get the feeling that as he speaks on television he must be laughing inside at this marvelous act he puts on. This is not to say that he does not have a high ego, for he does, but it is mostly for the public. He is really a very private man. He truly enjoys the bantering back and forth on television and does go out of his way to antagonize a few people, but he does so with the full knowledge that this is what the viewers want. As I said, he is a softy and wouldn't hurt a flea! He is also extremely generous. If you were a friend and in need, he would be the first in line to help. The need for harmony in his life is utmost, and he maintains a great show of harmony, even under the most trying circumstances.

In my opinion, he deserves the Emmy Award for best actor on television!

Barbara Walters, journalist, television correspondent.
The traits first—
Coarse hair 10, thick lips 8, turned-up nose 8, action eyelids 7, emotion 8, structured eyebrows 8 (also competitive 8), self-confidence 9, square forehead line 10, possessive 10, high cheekbones 10.

These combinations indicate a hard-working, dedicated professional in the business world. Her primary motivation is definitely recognition! The need to be recognized and accepted for *her* abilities is what drives her. At the same time she is an absolutely incurable romantic (thank goodness there are a few of us left!). She views things both competitively as well as structurally. Her mind runs to a well-organized pattern of thought; thus you will rarely catch her without something to say. If she is pausing in an interview, it is because she is in a thought process. The combination of action eyelids, coarse hair, and aggressive chin indicates that she literally operates at two speeds—faster than fast or asleep! Once she shuts the businesswoman off, she becomes a totally feminine woman, with all the needs of tenderness, romance, love, security (not financial), and caring that most of us dream about and want. In her case it would take a very sensitive yet strong man who would have to be very intelligent. One thing she does not want—and that is to have to compete with the man in her life romantically. She doesn't even want or desire to be the boss in the relationship, preferring to express her femininity. Often she comes across on television as cold and hard, but sincere and honest. On the business side this is very true; however, in the personal side only the sincerity and integrity remain. Her man would have to be warm and genuine, as well as completely honest.

She is, in my humble opinion, a very remarkable woman in our society, and her integrity is impeccable.

PRESIDENTS' TRAITS

1. President Ronald Reagan
(basic motivation: recognition of self)

Thin lips 10
Small irises 9
Partially closed eyes 9
Wedge-shaped chin 9
Roman nose 10
Square forehead line 10
Impulsive chin 9
Rhetoric lines 10
Possessive ears 9
Perfectionist's lines 0
Coarse hair 8
Forward ego balance 9
Dramatic-structured eyebrows 10

2. Jimmy Carter
(basic motivation: acceptance)

Analytical eyelids 10
Wide-open eyes 10
Large irises 10
Thick lips 10
Perfectionist's lines 10
Open-minded nose tip 10
Competitive eyebrows 10
Rounded or square chin 8
Square forehead line 10
Self-reliance 8
Self-confidence 10
Impulsive chin 2

3. Gerald Ford
(basic motivation: integrity—people)

Forward ego balance 10
Large irises 10
Wide-open eyes 6
Analytical eyelids 10
Flat eyebrows 9
Patience 10
Self-confidence 10
Structured organization 10
Rounded chin 8
Idealistic 10
Self-reliant 10

4. Richard Nixon
(basic motivation: power—recognition)

Small irises 8
Structured eyebrows 10
Skeptical nose tip 9
Helper's nose 10

Analytical eyelids 9
Wide-open eyes 5
Rounded or square chin 9
Tactful—public side 8, private 4
Curiosity 10
Rounded forehead line 8

5. Lyndon B. Johnson
(basic motivation: recognition)

Competitive eyebrows 10
Partially closed eyes 8
Skeptical nose tip 10
Money nose 10
Thin lips 8
Rounded forehead line 9
Possessive ears 9
Self-reliance—business 9, personal 4
Self-confidence 9
Rounded or square chin 10
Worry lines 10
Analytical eyelids—business 10, personal 7

6. John F. Kennedy
(basic motivation: recognition)

Analytical eyelids 10
Emotional eyes 9
Thick lips 9
Roman nose 10
Possessive ears 3
Humor lines 10
Rhetoric lines 10
Self-reliance 9
Self-confidence 10
Tact 9
Perfectionist lines 8
Coarse hair 10

7. **Dwight D. Eisenhower**

(basic motivation: integrity—people)

Wide-open eyes 10
Large irises 10
Skeptical nose tip 10
Self-reliance 10
Self-confidence 10
Analytical eyelids 10
Harmony eyebrows 10
Thin lips 8
Wedge-shaped chin 9
Rounded hairline 10

8. **Harry S. Truman**

(basic motivation: power—people)

Wedge-shaped chin 10
Thin lips 9
Skeptical nose tip 10
Price or Roman nose 10
Direct-action eyelids 7
Emotion 7
Wide-open eyes 10
Competitive eyebrows 10
Possessive ears 3
Impulsive chin 8
Self-confidence 10
Self-reliance 10
Ability to handle authority 10

Reference List
of Books

Fast, Julius. *Body Language.* New York: M. Evans & Co., 1970.

Kurtz, Ron and Prestera, Hector. *The Body Reveals.* New York: Harper & Row, 1976.

Lowen, Alexander. *Betrayal of the Body.* New York: Macmillan, 1969.

Mar, Timothy T. *Face Reading.* New York: New American Library, 1975.

Malloy, John T. *Dress for Success.* New York: David McKay, 1975.

Nierenberg, Gerald I. and Calero, Henry H. *How to Read a Person Like a Book.* New York: Hawthorn Books, 1971.

Scheflen, Albert E. *Body Language and the Social Order.* Englewood Cliffs, N. J.: Prentice-Hall, 1973.

Shirley, John. *Body Watching Is Fun.* Dallas: Taylor Publishing Co., 1973.

Whiteside, Robert. *Face Language.* New York: Frederick Fell, 1974.